PRAISE FOR
OUTSMART THE LEARNING CURVE

"Packed with compelling anecdotes and actionable science-backed advice, Sipher fills the gap between the hard-to-believe four-hour work week and the hard-to-achieve 10,000-hour approach to learning, success, and personal growth."

—Nicola Kraus, #1 *New York Times* bestselling author, over six million copies sold

"*Outsmart* illuminates a path to achievement often overlooked by a media focused on heroes du jour. Like a master chef, Sipher presents a clear recipe we can each season to taste to create our own exceptional life."

—Randy Komisar, bestselling author of *The Monk and the Riddle*, entrepreneur, investor, and university lecturer

"*Outsmart the Learning Curve* is not only a great read but also a practical guide that challenges conventional wisdom about self-improvement and personal growth—making what seems impossible feel within reach. Sipher gives us hope that just about anything is possible—empowering us to embrace rapid learning and giving us the courage to take on seemingly daunting challenges with confidence. He masterfully combines academic insight with real-world relevance, making *Outsmart the Learning Curve* inspiring from start to finish. This is a must-read for anyone seeking to unlock their full potential and make meaningful changes in their life."

—Kate Purmal, author of *Composure*, executive presence and leadership expert, fractional CxO, board director, and strategic advisor

"Through stories of relatable people with obstacle-laden life paths, this wonderful book outlines how anyone—but especially "regular" people—can become aligned with their authentic selves and find their way."

—Beth Wolff, therapist, licensed professional clinical counselor (LPCC)

"A game-changer for anyone looking to navigate the complexities of personal growth. Its practical strategies empower 'regular' people to tackle the often misunderstood challenges of learning and self-improvement. A must-read for anyone ready to embrace change and enhance their lives."

—Dr. Amelia Duran-Stanton, PhD, DSc, author of *The LOTUS Within: Grow Your Purpose and Ignite Your Passion*

"This is not your typical self-help book. *Outsmart the Learning Curve* is about the nuts and bolts of learning and using that knowledge to your advantage. Highly recommend!"

—David R. York, Esq., CPA author of *The Gift of Lift*

"Evidence-based yet easily digestible, Sipher's work is ahead of the curve. Essential reading for those committed to self-improvement."

—Irwin Epstein, Phd, Professor Emeritus, author of *Men as Friends: From Cicero to Svevo to Cataldo*

"This book shines as a departure from the myriad of self-development books that promise to help readers become their best selves but offer nothing new and fail to resonate with their sometimes tired and generic advice. Sipher masterfully connects, as readers will see themselves in many of the book's examples. This must-read is really a book about life and how our purpose is to know our best selves and beyond."

—Ryan Lindner, personal development specialist and author of *The Half-Known Life: What Matters Most When You're Running Out of Time*

"Joe Sipher's *Outsmart the Learning Curve* is a fast-paced, no-nonsense guidebook that profiles the journeys of ordinary people who were able to navigate significant obstacles to realize their passion. It provides concise, well-researched strategies, tools, and techniques that can help transform the ordinary into the extraordinary."

—Lori Pappas, entrepreneur, humanitarian, and author of *The Magic of Yes: Embrace the Wise Woman Within*

"As an author who has also woven science and stories together, I can tell you that Joe is a master! I especially appreciate how, instead of focusing on triggers, Joe shifts the focus to the more uplifting concept of glimmers, with practical, actionable advice at the end of every chapter. *Outsmart the Learning Curve* is a refreshing and valuable guide for anyone looking to grow."

— Madelaine Claire Weiss, bestselling author of *Getting to G.R.E.A.T.: 5-Step Strategy for Work and Life*

"Inspiring and actionable, *Outsmart the Learning Curve* is an exceptional self-help book designed to guide all people toward outstanding lives."

—*Foreword* Clarion Reviews

"Hopeful . . . relatable . . . grounded. I love the simplicity of it all—the imagery, the descriptions of the challenges, and the research findings."

—Lee Epting, executive presence coach, former Samsung and Vodafone executive

Outsmart the Learning Curve: How Ordinary People Can Achieve Extraordinary Success

by Joe Sipher

© Copyright 2024 Joe Sipher

ISBN 979-8-88824-547-7

All rights reserved. No part of this publication may be reproduced, stored in a retrieval system, or transmitted in any form or by any means—electronic, mechanical, photocopy, recording, or any other—except for brief quotations in printed reviews, without the prior written permission of the author.

Published by

3705 Shore Drive
Virginia Beach, VA 23455
800-435-4811
www.koehlerbooks.com

OUTSMART THE LEARNING CURVE

HOW ORDINARY PEOPLE CAN ACHIEVE EXTRAORDINARY SUCCESS

JOE SIPHER

VIRGINIA BEACH
CAPE CHARLES

For my father, Allen J. Sipher, who aspired to write a book but ran out of time way too early. This is an attempt to help fulfill your dream, Dad.

TABLE OF CONTENTS

INTRODUCTION 1
FIND YOUR GLIMMER 15
OPENNESS 44
GET HELP 72
CONFIDENCE 105
RESILIENCE 139
CONCLUSION 175
ACKNOWLEDGMENTS 179

INTRODUCTION

Avoid clichés like the plague.

—Smart alecks everywhere

PEOPLE LIKE ME CAN'T BE HERE

Martha Niño, an energetic, dedicated eighteen-year veteran of the software giant Adobe, volunteered one day to lead an elementary school tour of the company's gleaming campus. Martha enjoyed leading these tours because she loved interacting with the kids and showing off her workplace. This school was from Salinas, California, a city that may be best known as the hometown of famed novelist John Steinbeck, who featured it in classics such as *East of Eden*, *Grapes of Wrath*, and *Of Mice and Men*. Today, Salinas is known as the "Salad Bowl of the World," given its high output of crops like lettuce, spinach, broccoli, and strawberries. Salinas also has the highest proportion of Hispanic Americans in any California city.[1] Nearly 80 percent of its citizens are Hispanic, many of whom are undocumented immigrants.

Martha guided the Salinas elementary students through the pristine Adobe campus, featuring a freshly painted basketball court, a state-of-the-art gym, and refrigerators fully stocked with unlimited free drinks. These perks, which many white-collar workers take for granted, were absolutely eye-popping for these children whose parents may have worked for poverty wages in Salinas strawberry fields.

Toward the end of the tour, Martha noticed one boy's eyes start to water. Martha asked, "What's wrong, sweetheart?"

The teary-eyed boy slowly quivered. "This is great, but people like me can't be here." Martha deeply understood the boy's pain. He saw no hope in his future, only the poverty and hard labor that surrounded him at home. At that moment, Martha realized she needed to break a vow of silence she had maintained for forty-seven years.

People who come to the United States as undocumented immigrants are told from an early age to stay quiet, do what they're told, and not answer questions about their background. Even though Martha had received her green card more than thirty years earlier, she never told her wrenching immigrant story to anyone. But she saw that deeply shameful part of herself in that boy. She knelt down, lifted the boy's chin until their teary eyes met, and softly said, "I *am* you." For the first time, Martha shared how similar her childhood was to this boy's, and despite her humble start, she became a successful manager at a global corporation.

Martha's story of going from barely surviving on a Mexican cotton farm to thriving in corporate America embodies the essence of this book. How does anyone overcome incredible obstacles to make life transformations? One way to think about it is that they simply have to learn. They must learn new approaches, skills, and methods for success. And we're not just talking about academic learning. Martha had to learn a new culture, a new language, the laws of her new country, and how to navigate her world socially as an undocumented immigrant. Her parents were little help as they barely knew more than she did. Her father dropped out of school after second grade to support his family, and her mother only managed to get through sixth grade.

How did Martha navigate these circumstances differently from so many others in her position? Did she have some secret to learning and coping with adversity that others didn't? She did, and this book will describe techniques and strategies that Martha and several other ordinary people used to make extraordinary transformations or work through adversity. It also includes science-backed research to support how these people succeeded, which will give you the confidence to apply the same techniques to your unique circumstances. While the stories and research in this book lean toward career-oriented issues, the tools and techniques can help you through any type of transformation or form of adversity, whether it's career-oriented, health-oriented, or life-oriented.

WHY THIS BOOK IS DIFFERENT

Of course, there are countless books about self-development, success, and learning. Many of the ones I find myself reading, such as *Outliers*, *Grit*, and *Talent Is Overrated*, describe how world-class people became world-class. While they are excellent, inspirational books, I suspect many people buy them in hopes of finding a way to make *themselves* better. Not long ago, I downloaded a new book that I didn't initially recognize as part of the genre. Quickly, it started quoting studies about 10,000 hours of deliberate practice[*] and how the author became the top table tennis player in the UK. At that moment, I thought, *I'm never going to be a world-class anything. Why am I reading this book? What I want is a book about how regular people can improve and succeed.*

---

[*] We'll talk more about practice later, but the 10,000 hours rule states that to become an expert, people require 10,000 hours of deliberate practice focused on that skill. Originally reported by Florida State University Professor of Psychology Anders Ericsson, this idea was popularized by Malcom Gladwell's *Outliers* and is referred to *ad nauseum* in many "success" books.

When I couldn't find a book like that, I decided to write this one—to provide accessible, achievable, and practical solutions for non-world-class people like me and 99.9 percent of you (Roger Federer and Bill Gates, you can stop reading now). This book is both for "regular" people and about "regular" people you are unlikely to recognize, like Martha Niño. That said, in many ways, each person covered here is even more inspiring than the world-class usual suspects, simply because none of them were gifted with top 0.1 percent natural abilities, nor, by and large, did they have parents who optimized for their success by methodically planning every step of their early years. In fact, many of the people profiled here had difficult starts or, at best, ordinary childhoods. Yet, somewhere along the way, each made an inspiring, dramatic transformation that is both instructive and fascinating for anyone who wants to achieve something similar. After researching hundreds of people, I narrowed the subjects to these seven, who represent a wide range of experiences and backgrounds, but all found surprising success in their own contexts. In the following pages, you'll meet

- Isabel Cardoso, a marketing manager with no math or science background, who, at thirty-six, made the improbable leap to aerospace engineer and now works on the Orion moon exploration spacecraft at Lockheed Martin.

- Helen Wells, who was dissuaded from following her passion for art at seventeen, was rejected from art school at twenty-nine, and after another decade, finally quit her day job to become a completely self-supporting artist.

- Jason Lee, whose parents drilled into him since early childhood that he would become a doctor. A struggle with organic chemistry coupled with a vision that came to him during a concert led to this twenty-six-year-old running an eight-figure real estate business.

- Jeremy Schifeling, who went from a failing kindergarten teacher to a sought-after consultant at Harvard, Stanford, and nearly every top MBA program in the world.

- Chase Friedman, a buoyant twenty-five-year-old who was paralyzed in a freak accident and stunned doctors with his amazing recovery.

- Jason Christie, a promising "golden child" of medical research who somehow failed on his first seven attempts to get NIH grant funding before making a career out of life-saving contributions to the field of lung transplantation.

- Martha Niño, the amazing woman you just met, who made the incredible journey from a silenced undocumented immigrant to a trusted Fortune 500 manager, published author, accomplished public speaker, and creator of her own foundation dedicated to giving hope to immigrant students.

You'll also be reading a little about me, a rudderless English major fired from his first job for incompetence. This aimless, unemployed twenty-two-year-old, who had steered clear of STEM classes, somehow worked himself into a foundational product management job at Palm, later started two profitable mobile app companies, and was granted twenty-six patents related to mobile technology, wireless communications, and user interface design. Like the other people profiled in this book, I'm just a regular person who made a transformation to success through a combination of luck, hard work, and being clever in my approach to life's inevitable obstacles. It's the last clever bit that I want to share.

The journeys of the people in this book demonstrate that, with the right mindset, strategies, and perseverance, we all have the ability to achieve remarkable things. My hope is that their stories and the supporting research that validates their approaches will motivate you to believe in your own capacity for self-development and give you the tools to overcome obstacles or make dramatic transformations. Like the people profiled here, you have the power to become the best version of yourself by outsmarting the learning curve.

THE LEARNING CURVE

To find success where there has only been failure, you have to change something. Change requires learning—learning new approaches, new techniques, or new ways of thinking about the problem. This book is about how you can change yourself to get better career-wise, socially, athletically, or just in general. If you're going to make substantial or even dramatic changes to your life, you need top-notch learning techniques to match. Education theorists and psychologists have studied learning for centuries, and one of the tools they developed to track how people learn a particular skill or set of skills is the learning curve. As simple as the learning curve sounds, it is a widely misunderstood measure.

A classic learning curve follows an S-shaped pattern where the vertical axis measures skill proficiency, and the horizontal axis represents time, as shown in the graphic below. This S-shaped pattern for human learning has been replicated countless times in scientific studies, measuring everything from the productivity of Croatian harvest machine operators[2] to British ultrasound trainees[3] to New Zealander colonoscopists.[4] The S-shaped learning curve is not controversial; it simply illustrates the way humans learn new skills over time.

The misunderstood aspect of the learning curve relates to the common cautionary warning "That has a steep learning curve." What does that really mean? While the phrase "steep learning curve" is often used to describe a skill that is difficult to learn, if you spend a moment studying the graph below, it's clear that the exact opposite is true—the steeper the curve, the *faster* the learning. The phrase "steep learning curve" is a deeply rooted misnomer in our culture. I'm not the first to make this observation, but this may be the first book that delves into how to leverage the power and intricacies of learning curves for personal growth.

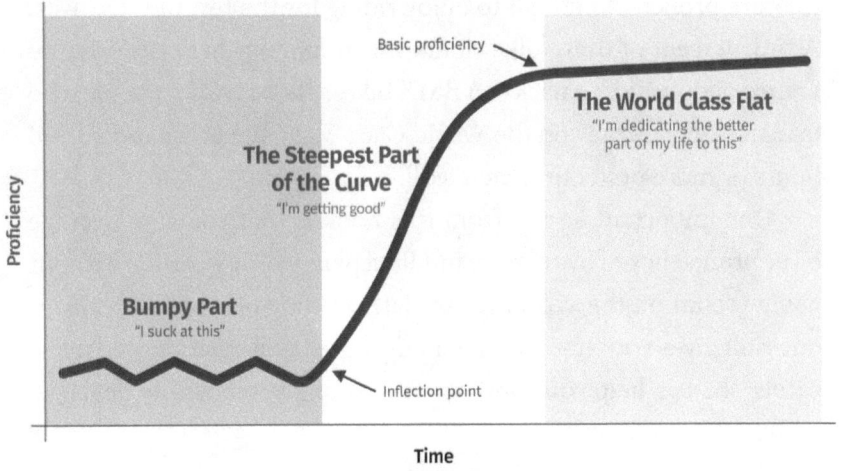

Figure 1—The Learning Curve

You've already experienced this positive interpretation of speeding up a steep learning curve many times in your life. A common example is learning to ride a bicycle. I taught my three kids to ride a bike. The day those training wheels came off, there was a lot of fear and a complete lack of understanding of how it all worked. Some kids say they don't want to learn to ride or just want to keep the training wheels on. What they may be feeling is a bit of fear and "I suck at this." They are experiencing the seemingly endless Bumpy Part of the learning curve, as shown above.

After minutes, days, or weeks of bumpy trial, the bike learner hits an inflection point: the moment they start pedaling forward with force while simultaneously using the handlebars for balance. Aha! The fun part! From that "inflection point" to confidently riding around the neighborhood usually takes less than an hour. Those few minutes are the Steepest Part of the learning curve, when something "clicks" and learning is easiest.

At some point, soon after getting through the Steepest Part, most people stop getting significantly better at riding a bike. Yet they are proficient enough to enjoy riding for the rest of their lives. A tiny percent of those bike riders will go on to ride in the Tour de France or do amazing tricks on BMX bikes. Those are the people who take the long journey on the World Class Flat and may spend 10,000 hours or more perfecting their skill.

One important lesson from this book is that you can leverage basic proficiency to live a more fulfilling personal or work life without going too far on the World Class Flat. Leveling off at proficiency in one skill gives you time to learn many other skills that may enable a career change, help you overcome a seemingly impossible obstacle, or just bring you joy.

JUMPING CURVES

If we extend this learning curve model a little further, we can apply it to a broader range of skill learning. For example, to accomplish a major transformation or learn a completely new vocation, you'll likely be faced with multiple learning curves. Some of these curves will be parallel to each other. For example, in starting a business, one curve might be about understanding customer needs, and another completely different curve may be about how to create a successful business model.

Just as likely, improving skills more deeply may require working through learning curves that will be sequential in nature. Once you reach proficiency on one curve or skill, for example, riding a bike on pavement, you may be able to jump to a completely different but related curve—like mountain biking. The mountain biking curve requires learning deeper skills involving braking and shifting gears while riding on uneven or unstable terrain. Most people can't jump directly to a more advanced curve like mountain biking without first going through the basic bike riding curve.

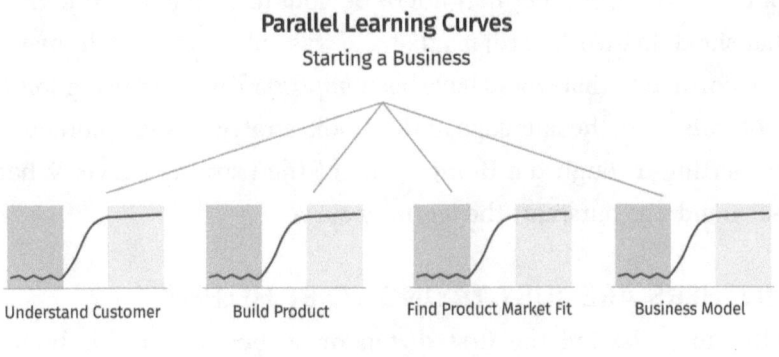

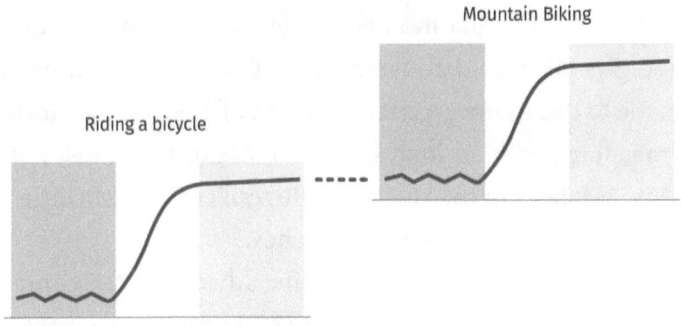

Figure 2—Parallel and Sequential Learning Curves

GET TO THE STEEPEST PART OF THE CURVE

This book is largely about how to get through the Bumpy Part of the learning curve. That's what people really mean when they say that a skill has a "steep learning curve." In the context of this book, that means it's difficult to get to the inflection point. When initially hearing this learning curve concept, one of the subjects of the book, Isabel, said, "But there are no shortcuts." Of course, in many ways, she's right. She had to work hard and persevere in the face of notable adversity to make her transformation. While Isabel didn't feel like she was taking shortcuts, her story is filled with shortcuts and strategies that enabled her to make her transformation. Some of these came naturally to her, but they may not be obvious to everyone else. It's not that she didn't work hard; it's that she was able to make a dramatic transformation that would have been *impossible* without using some shortcuts or, in the language of this book, strategies and techniques for getting through the Bumpy Part of the learning curve. What Isabel did was outsmart the learning curve.

MOTHERS ARE JUST TRYING TO BE HELPFUL

After interviewing the first dozen or so people for this book, clear patterns started emerging. Even though the subjects came from widely different backgrounds and made a variety of different transformations, the aha moments, the inflection points, and the key strategies all started converging. But when I started trying to put a name to these convergent ideas, they all boiled down to advice a well-meaning parent or high school counselor might toss out: "Be confident," "Make your own luck," or "Be resilient." There's little value in a book that regurgitates success clichés.

Of course, the hard part is executing advice like "be confident." How exactly might a self-doubting person become more confident? What does it mean to make your own luck? Is there a way to become more resilient in the face of adversity?

That's why this book will not only explore what to do but also provide practical guidance about *how* to do it based on the experiences of some ordinary people who made amazing transformations and a plethora of supporting research showing how these ideas can be applied more broadly. The end of each chapter includes actionable, bulleted recommendations for making progress. In addition, there's a free, downloadable workbook at www.outsmartbook.com/workbook that goes beyond the end-of-chapter bullets and gives you space for more open-ended reflection on how the topics relate to your world and helpful exercises to reinforce the concepts.

BOOK ROADMAP

The rest of the book is structured into five chapters. Here's a preview of each:

1. **Find Your Glimmer.** Before outsmarting a learning curve, each of the subjects in this book had to decide which overarching curve to invest in. This decision starts with a glimmer, the feeling that draws you to a subject area or activity. This chapter helps you identify your own glimmer and how to develop it into the purpose that will drive you forward.

2. **Openness.** Perhaps the most surprising finding in this book was that an attitude of openness was critical for people getting through the Bumpy Part of the learning curve. An almost carefree openness to follow new paths, view problems in a unique way, or meet new people enabled their transformations. This chapter defines the openness personality trait from an academic point of view and from a real-world perspective. It goes on to describe methods you can use to improve your level of openness to achieve better outcomes.

3. **Get Help.** Asking for help is an obvious way to shortcut the Bumpy Part of the curve. Going it alone may feel heroic in the moment, but you won't get as far as someone who gets help from others. This chapter explores how to cultivate a support system of believers, mentors, and peers who can provide opportunities, advice, and accountability. It covers the best ways to leverage your network, how to overcome barriers to asking for help, and approaches to surrounding yourself with experienced people who can accelerate your learning. You'll also learn how welcoming help from casual acquaintances and unexpected sources can lead to surprising breakthroughs.

4. **Confidence.** Confidence can help with almost every human interaction. But how does a self-doubting person become more confident? This chapter describes several techniques for gaining confidence, such as how to maintain positivity in the face of daunting odds and how well-studied practice techniques can help you build confidence to get through the Bumpy Part of the learning curve. You'll also learn how it's possible to become more extroverted (whether you're an introvert or an extrovert) and the value that increased extroversion provides to your well-being and ability.

5. **Resilience.** Resilience usually means having the grit, determination, and will to face adversity (the Bumpy Part of the learning curve). All that's true, but this chapter provides tools to make resilience easier and success more achievable when confronted with daunting obstacles. You'll learn to use tools like humor, gratitude, and a supportive environment to build resilience. You'll also learn how to predict whether your continued failures will eventually lead to success or if it's time to quit.

INTRODUCTION SUMMARY

- This book is for "regular" people and about "regular" people. This inclusive approach enables nearly anyone to apply the book's concepts.

- A central theme of the book is how you can change yourself to get better career-wise, socially, athletically, or just in general. Change requires learning, and how people learn is often misunderstood.

- The term "steep learning curve" is a deeply rooted misnomer. The hard stuff happens before the steepest part of the curve.

- The book's primary focus is sharing techniques and strategies for getting through the Bumpy Part of the curve, up to the inflection point. If you can get to the inflection point, learning happens quickly.

- Leveling off at basic proficiency in one skill gives you time to learn more skills that may enable a career change, help overcome a seemingly impossible obstacle, or simply enrich your life.

- Expanding on the learning curve model, the curves can be parallel or sequential; mastering one enables moving to the next. You will likely need to address multiple learning curves for a major transformation or to overcome an obstacle.

CHAPTER 1
FIND YOUR GLIMMER

The only way to do great work is to love what you do. If you haven't found it yet, keep looking. Don't settle.
—Steve Jobs

ISABEL'S MEANDERING START

Isabel Cardoso[*] was fifteen years into a productive marketing career when, at thirty-six, she decided to make the seemingly ridiculous career move to become an aerospace engineer. Starting with essentially high school level math and science, Isabel fought through all the prerequisite calculus and physics, earned a master's in aerospace engineering, and bagged a coveted systems engineering job at Lockheed Martin on the Orion spacecraft used for the Artemis moon exploration program. Isabel transformed her career in a way that you rarely hear about. Paradoxically, her early life resembled a leaf blowing in the wind, not a focused, purposeful march to an end goal. How did Isabel's somewhat aimless beginnings develop into such a disciplined, focused career?

Isabel's family immigrated to the US from Brazil when she was eight. Between third and eleventh grade, her family moved *nine*

---

[*] To protect her privacy, Isabel's name and select details of her story have been changed, without compromising the integrity of her remarkable journey.

times—so often that, until she reached her junior year in high school, Isabel never finished the year at the same school she started. Think about that. Isabel was always coming in midyear as the new kid. "It was just a constant. You come home one day and get told that, by the way, we're moving again."

In her first year or two in the US, Isabel barely spoke English. Even as she picked up the language, the frequent moves prevented her from making deep friendships or joining sports teams (tryouts always seemed to have happened already), and they required her to constantly acclimate to new academic rules, systems, and measures. Until her junior year, with each move, she just "rolled with it." However, the last move really hurt, as she had started building friendships, and as Isabel points out, "High school is a time when you really need your friends." At that point, her family had settled in the Houston, Texas, area. Here, Isabel spent the next twenty years figuring out what she wanted to do.

Isabel's home life was complicated by her parents' divorce. By the time she was ready for college, her parents weren't able to pay, and eighteen-year-old Isabel couldn't comprehend getting $100,000 in loans for a degree from well-respected private Rice University, where she had been admitted as a freshman. Instead, she worked through college, cobbling together credits between the University of Houston and community college. In the end, earning her BS in business administration extended to five and a half years largely because work often had to take precedence over school.

To make ends meet, Isabel continued her high school job at the local Randalls, then moved on to become an executive assistant for a software company. Toward the end of undergrad, Isabel started working in the marketing department of that same company, where she got her first taste of that field.

Three months after "barely passing" with a BS in business from the University of Houston, Isabel took a project manager job in a startup founded by a team she had worked with earlier. This was the go-go days of the 1999 dot-com explosion, and her company was doing a lot of acquisitions. Isabel's job was to project manage the integration of the acquired companies into the mothership. Quickly, she saw that the people who were doing the truly interesting work all had MBAs. Only three months after graduating, being able to deposit a steady paycheck and having enough money "to buy any cheese I wanted," she decided to go back to school and get an MBA.

By the time Isabel finished her MBA, the dot-com crash of 2001 was dragging the economy down, and she struggled to find a full-time job. In hopes of digging up a lead or learning something new, she attended an event at the University of Houston intended to help "emerging leaders grow and develop." The speaker "waxed on about following your heart and doing what you love, blah, blah, blah. So I raised my hand."

Isabel asked the presenter, "What if you have to follow your heart *and* you gotta pay your rent?"

The speaker, former C-level executive, consultant, and board member Margot Dufresne, said, "Sometimes the answer is right in front of your face."

Isabel jokingly waved her hands in front of her face, miming that she couldn't find anything. The audience laughed, and Margot encouraged Isabel to follow up with her after the session.

That night, Isabel went to work on a PowerPoint called "HelpYouHelpMe.ppt," which she thoughtfully created to give Margot insight into her background and make Margot's offer to help easier. Margot was so impressed with Isabel's PowerPoint that she hired her, on a contract basis, to help with startup ideas she was working on. This was one more leg in Isabel's meandering journey—but a fortuitous one.

WHAT DOES GLIMMER MEAN?

This book focuses on describing techniques and strategies to get through the Bumpy Part of the learning curve. But first, it's important to understand what macro learning curve you want to invest all that time and energy into. Strategically, what are you going to be working toward, and why? Just figuring that out can be a pretty instructive process. If you think you've already found your purpose in life and want to skip ahead, this chapter is still worth a read. First, you'll want to understand the origin stories of the subjects profiled later in the book. And perhaps more importantly, this chapter may help you realize there's something else, a glimmer that's been inside you all along.

• • •

Up to this point, Isabel seemed to have been making snap decisions that have long-term consequences with relatively little data. She seemed to be running but not toward anything in particular. Seemingly reflective of her childhood, Isabel moved from one opportunity to another as possibilities presented themselves. She wasn't strategic about her career and life decisions. Yet her approach may, in fact, have been the most effective in her quest to find her "glimmer."

I define "glimmer" as a strong feeling that draws you to a subject area, approach, or activity that you really care about. A glimmer is a vague feeling that ideally will graduate to your "purpose." For me, at about fourteen or fifteen, my glimmer was "computers." I didn't know what else to call this satisfying feeling I got when I tinkered with them, learned about them, and programmed them for a couple of summers. In my free time, I read computer magazines and even software manuals cover-to-cover to learn how software programs work. Mistakenly assuming the only vocation for people like me was computer programming and realizing that I didn't want to sit in front of a screen and code all day, I decided to make "computers" my hobby until I realized the career of product management was my purpose. I didn't even understand what a product manager was until I was twenty-eight years old.

• • •

Isabel hadn't discovered her glimmer yet, let alone her purpose. Through research and my own interviews, I divided people yet to find their purpose into one of three camps:

1. People who somewhat aimlessly bounce from one thing to another until they finally find their purpose or get stuck in their last experiment.

2. People who have a glimmer buried inside them but don't think they have time, money, or enough skill to focus on it or may be worried that people will judge them if they pursue it and fail.

3. People who stopped exploring a bit too early, often because they were driven down a path of expectation, sometimes by parents.

We'll see examples of people in camps two and three later, but let's get back to Isabel, who was clearly in the first camp—"explore mode"—during this part of her career.

ARE YOU A MAXIMIZER OR A SATISFICER?

It turns out there is interesting research indicating Isabel's exploratory method yields higher job satisfaction for job searchers than those who try to finalize the "perfect" job too early. A Columbia/Swarthmore study[5] surveyed hundreds of graduating college seniors and sorted them into two groups based on earlier seminal choice-making research: *maximizers* and *satisficers*.[6] Maximizers are people who, in modern terms, are the type to spend a long time looking for the perfect Netflix show and end up with perhaps a better one, though with less time to watch it. In contrast, satisficers would more likely look for something "good enough" on Netflix, watch sooner, and therefore have more time for the actual content.

After classifying these graduating seniors as either maximizers or satisficers using a preliminary survey, the researchers followed up with them after they had landed their first job out of college. While the maximizers' average salary was 20 percent higher than the satisficers, the satisficers were 8 percent happier with their jobs than the maximizers. The authors of the study theorized that maximizers were less satisfied because their pursuit of the elusive "best" option caused them to consider many more possibilities than the satisficers. The greater number of options increased their potential for unrealistically high expectations and caused rumination about brain-stretching opportunity costs—*I wonder if I would have been better off with that job I turned down.*

I have not found a follow-up study on these subjects, but I suspect there's a mismatch between what a young version of a person pursues and what the older version of that same person realizes they want later in life. If you ask twelve-year-olds what they want to be when they grow up, their answer likely won't line up with their interests at twenty-two. Following that logic, would a twenty-two-year-old's ideas about the perfect career path line up with their thirty-two-year-old self? That's why the "explore mode" that Isabel followed may have ultimately offered her the best possibility of finding her glimmer.

However, executing in explore mode can get you into trouble, depending on how you do it. A 2021 Harris Poll of 1,000 US adults aged thirty-three to forty found that nearly half the respondents regretted their career path when starting out.[7] The survey reported that many wish they had more guidance on choosing a career that matched their interests with the job market.

Other regrets include

- not taking enough risks early in their careers
- not trying different fields
- staying too long in unsatisfying jobs due to financial constraints.

The Harris Poll about unsatisfied millennials and the Columbia/Swarthmore study of maximizers and satisficers point to the same conclusion: young adults should spend a few years out of college figuring out what they really want to do by trying new things, knowing that the goal is to find their glimmer, vocation, or purpose—not trying to find the elusive "perfect" job. Similarly, people who've made a career choice as a twenty-something can and should be in explore mode, particularly if they realize that the path they're on is not fulfilling.

EXPLORE MODE MAY NOT BE COMFORTABLE

Isabel's approach to her career is the opposite of what Western culture drives young people toward. By putting students on "tracks" as early as elementary school and requiring them to select college majors early, school systems are set up to increase urgency in career planning as well as make young people feel like they can't go back on a decision they made. Even the term "undecided" for college students who haven't declared a major contributes to the negative connotation for those still discovering who they are and what they're interested in. A University of Maryland study of 3,091 incoming college freshmen[8] found that those who reportedly found their calling (roughly what we're calling purpose here) were more likely to feel confident with their career path, understand themselves better, and see work as highly important to their identity. The freshmen who said they were still searching for their calling reported that they were more indecisive and less comfortable with their career outlook. Of course, they were.

When your eighteen-year-old peers have confidently decided to become a cardiologist, nonprofit lawyer, or environmental engineer, and you haven't a clue what you want to do for your career, that applies some pressure. The undecided feel "behind" their peers and perhaps much more anxious about their careers. However, if incoming freshmen take the mindset that college is a time to *find* their glimmer versus assuming they know it, I suspect they'll be more comfortable and more likely to find something they truly care about. Further, I would argue many of those incoming freshmen who claimed they knew their calling as eighteen-year-olds were exuding false confidence. There are almost certainly interests, curiosities, and career options they never knew about or considered, but now they are on a seemingly permanent path. In twenty years, these overconfident freshmen may feel similarly to the Harris Poll subjects who didn't spend enough time choosing a degree/career that matched their interests and the job market.

ISABEL SEES A GLIMMER

One of the startup ideas Margot Dufresne asked Isabel to work on was a software tool for marketing professionals. Margot called in another senior businesswoman to help with the idea, Eleanor Chen, who had a long and successful career in marketing and was also looking for her next big thing. The three women agreed to meet at Isabel's house to discuss the new business idea.

This mundane meeting changed Isabel's life forever.

Eleanor arrived a little late and made a joke about how it would have been faster for her to fly to Houston from her home in Conroe, normally about an hour's drive. In the post-joke chatter between Margot and Eleanor, Isabel realized that Eleanor was only half joking—she really was a pilot. "It was the first time I met someone who flew for fun, who was female. I didn't know [regular] people flew airplanes. And that was basically the beginning of [me wanting to] learn how to fly."

Nothing ever came of that startup idea, and Isabel never met Eleanor in person again. But the idea of a female pilot was so inspiring to twenty-five-year-old Isabel Cardoso that she vowed to save up enough so she could take flying lessons one day. The glimmer started to glow, but it would take Isabel nearly two decades to realize how it would evolve into her purpose.

To save enough money to take flying lessons, Isabel embarked on a career in marketing games. While working for Margot, she had done some research showing that more people stay home and play video games during economic downturns. What better time to get into games than the depths of the dot-com crash? The only problem was that Isabel really wasn't a gamer and barely knew the first thing about games. Worse yet, as Isabel described, "The thing with games is that the best way to get into games is to be in games. It's just this very insular community."

Pivoting to game marketing illustrates how Isabel was following the satisficer strategy, jumping to a new opportunity without spending too much time analyzing it. Was it clear her generalized theory about more people playing games in a downturn could be translated into a long-term business opportunity? Not really. Was game marketing a career choice that perfectly matched her interests with job market opportunities? Honestly, no. But she wasn't exactly sure where her interests lay, and if she gave the game industry a chance, maybe it would prove to be a lifelong passion.

So Isabel perused Craigslist for an opportunity to get her foot in the door. She found a post by a game company to update their website. There were just two problems: 1) the website used a finicky technology that Isabel didn't know called Flash,[9] and 2) the company didn't have the budget for the update and asked if anyone would do it for free. Any self-respecting Flash developer would never do it for free, but Isabel volunteered for the job to learn Flash and, more importantly, be able to add something game-related to her résumé. She fought her way through understanding enough Flash to make the update. As Isabel said, "There was no joy in it, but it was a means to an end."

The hiring manager for the Flash project, Debra Rossini, was so impressed with Isabel's work that she wondered what else Isabel might be able to help her with. Isabel was looking to build her résumé for a paying job, so she asked for projects requiring her to learn new skills to help her break into the games industry. It was a symbiotic relationship where Debra would get lots of little projects done for free, and Isabel was able to acquire several game marketing skills to punch up her résumé. We'll revisit Isabel's strategy of using free labor as a clever way to gain experience while mitigating risk in the "Openness" chapter.

ISABEL KEEPS HER GLIMMER WARM WHILE PAYING THE RENT

While completing small projects for Debra, Isabel continued her full-time job search. After a couple of dry months during the depths of the early 2000s recession, Isabel found an ad for a summer internship at Mac game publisher Aspyr Media. If you've never heard of Aspyr Media, you might know one or two of their blockbuster Mac game properties, such as *Tomb Raider*, *Tony Hawk*, or *Star Wars*. As an MBA graduate, Isabel was overqualified for a summer internship, but this was an opportunity to get on the inside of one of the most important game companies in the industry.

Isabel spent hours looking for the hiring manager's name on the internet and then dug up the lone video interview the guy gave. She just wanted to get a sense of him. Isabel then spent two hours composing, editing, and reediting a cold email to get the interview. And she got it!

Now what? Isabel really wasn't a gamer and didn't even own a Mac. But she needed a way to stand out. With barely any money in her checking account, Isabel used a credit card to buy a used Mac she couldn't afford. Isabel knew that the hiring manager had worked on the *Spiderman* game, so she bought the latest version on credit as well.

With a Mac and the *Spiderman* game in hand, Isabel was still somewhat at a loss. She had no idea how to assess a game. So she went back to Debra Rossini and asked for help. Debra rattled off a series of standard criteria to evaluate games while Isabel diligently wrote down every word she could catch. As you'll see in the "Get Help" chapter, the value of asking for help from strangers, loose connections, colleagues, or friends is another critical strategy for quickly moving past the Bumpy Part of the curve. Isabel knew that intuitively (maybe we all do), but unlike many, she wasn't afraid to ask.

Then, not having seriously played a game since she was fourteen, Isabel worked through the entirety of *Spiderman*. While she didn't know much about games, her MBA taught her some basic skills on how to acquire customer feedback. In theory, those skills transferred to the gaming world, so she put together a survey for *Spiderman* players that allowed them to evaluate the game based on the criteria that Debra had provided. Then she posted the survey on Craigslist and built a crisp PowerPoint summarizing the results. She had this summary in hand for her first interview.

Isabel didn't know it at the time, but Ivy League MBA candidates were competing with her for this coveted summer internship. After a positive interview highlighted by Isabel's *Spiderman* game survey summary, the hiring manager worked hard to ensure Isabel got the internship. "He selected me over all these incredible people because he was like, they're all cocky . . . and you showed you were willing to work." Her manager at Aspyr converted the job from a summer intern to a contractor, which tripled the pay and essentially kicked off Isabel's career in game marketing. She had gotten her foot in the door. After a few years working her way up at Aspyr, she moved to another game company and later spent eight years as a marketing manager at web hosting company HostGator.

ISABEL'S GLIMMER BRIGHTENS

But of course, all this marketing stuff was a means to an end. It wasn't that Isabel didn't enjoy learning game marketing from the brilliant minds at Aspyr Media or spreading the word about cost-effective web hosting at HostGator. In fact, she was passionate about the companies she worked for and the products she marketed. Yet this deep desire to fly, sparked from that one meeting with Eleanor Chen, was burning inside her. After twelve years, she finally had the funds to pay for her first flying lesson in 2014, and she absolutely loved it.

According to Isabel, there are essentially two aspects to flight school: "desk stuff," where students learn the basics in a classroom, and "air stuff," which is when you get to fly a real plane with a flight instructor. Most people drudge through the desk stuff so they can get to the air stuff. But Isabel absolutely loved the desk stuff too. The primary textbook for the desk stuff is the *Pilot's Handbook of Aeronautical Knowledge*. This book provides aspiring pilots with everything they need to understand aerodynamic theory and the practical aspects of flying. Isabel absorbed it all easily.

More surprising to her was that some of her classmates struggled with the aerodynamic theory parts of flight school. She remembers one person who had taken the class three times and still didn't get the aerodynamics material. "This woman had no idea how an airplane engine worked." Isabel didn't think it was that hard, so she confidently said, "I'm going to show you in ten minutes." She walked up to the whiteboard and started drawing all the components of an airplane engine and explaining how each part interacted with the others. Then her classmate started asking questions about these "unimportant things." Isabel realized that instead of understanding the flow and interaction between parts of the engine, her classmate mostly seemed to be trying to memorize what individual components were called. She couldn't pick out what was important from what was not or how the components worked together as a system.

It dawned on Isabel that understanding that flow came easily to her. "I don't have a photographic memory, but I understood the systems really well—far beyond what is actually necessary to fly." With that deeper understanding of how an airplane engine worked, she also intuitively understood what would happen if any of those parts failed—important if you're mid-flight and something goes wrong. It was at this moment that Isabel recognized that she had a latent engineering talent that had been there all along.

"And so I was like, huh, I think there's something here, but I really tried to let it go because I had a life. I had a mortgage. I had a career. I really was not trying to completely uproot my life in this crazy way . . . but the thing was, I couldn't let it go. There was this magnetic attraction that just kept coming back." This inability to "let it go" is a pretty clear signal that Isabel had found her glimmer. If something just keeps coming back to you, and you can't let it go, you owe it to yourself to pursue it.

Of course, it's risky to make that leap of faith. We'll learn how Isabel went from a career marketing manager to an aerospace engineer soon. But I want to get back to the three camps of people finding their glimmer. Let's shift to Helen, our camp-two representative, who had a glimmer glowing from a young age but kept running into walls as she attempted to turn her glimmer into a purpose.

I WAS ALWAYS AN ARTY KID

Helen Wells is a colorful woman in every sense of the word. The first time we Zoomed between her UK studio and my home office in San Francisco, her intensely colorful presence jumped through the broadband. It started at the top, with her red hair held back by a vividly patterned scarf tied in an artful bow. Her color sense also came through on that call, from her clever use of language to the cacophony of books, art, and knickknacks on her bookshelf to the freshly painted abstract behind her, which was filled with pleasing shapes and bathed in rich, radiant tones. Her Zoom appearance communicated a lot about Helen: a talented artist who deeply understands who she is and how to market herself. Unlike Isabel, Helen's glimmer was glowing from an early age. However, it took nearly twenty years of frustration, self-doubt, and resilience to become a full-time, self-supporting artist.

Helen was raised in a small town north of London, the youngest of three children. She was "quite an arty kid" growing up in quite an arty house. Helen remembers being encouraged to draw, color, and explore a wide variety of arts and crafts throughout her early years. Artfulness ran in the family, too, with her mother's creative embroidery sprinkled all over her childhood home. Helen loved "doing art" and showed some innate creative talent all the way through high school. But in the Wells household, art was just a hobby—all the children were encouraged from an early age to have a "proper" job. It was even more important for Helen as a girl because her parents wanted to ensure she found a career that would enable her to support herself.

So at seventeen, Helen, the girl who loved art, gave it up completely.

In the UK, students must pass at least three "A level" exams in their final two years of preparatory school to get into university. While art and design are one of many subject areas offered through the A-level system, neither her parents nor the school system encouraged that particular track. "If you're bright, you shouldn't really be doing art" was the message Helen received. So she chose more academically oriented subjects for her A-levels and ended up going to university for journalism. After graduating, she went on to get a postgraduate degree in public and media relations, which led to a six-year public relations career with a boutique consumer PR firm in London.

Public relations wasn't fulfilling enough for Helen, though. She wanted to add value in a more meaningful way. She wanted to feel *good* about what she was contributing to the world. So, Helen decided to change her career path and focus on a charitable organization. She found a role working for the nonprofit organization Business in the Community, a charity that encourages businesses to be greener and fairer to all their constituents. She started near the bottom of the career ladder, but ten years later, she found herself as the director of the Workplace Gender Equality practice, an important role where she managed a big team and was doing good for the world. But that wasn't enough. "It got to a point where I thought, *I'm not sure this is the life I want.*"

HELEN'S VENN DIAGRAM OF PURPOSE

During that first colorful Zoom call, Helen mentioned in passing the idea that when looking for a career, there should be "a kind of Venn diagram [that includes] things you love, things that make money, and things that other people find useful." I found that model a simple yet profound way to describe the criteria for finding one's true purpose.

After our chat, I researched the idea a bit more and discovered something similar, referred to as the *ikigai* model. This concept, rooted in Japanese philosophy, includes a fourth element: "things you're good at." But you can change what you're good at—that's what this book is all about. So, I like Helen's version better, which does not include the "things you're good at" bubble, though I changed her term "useful" to "valuable."

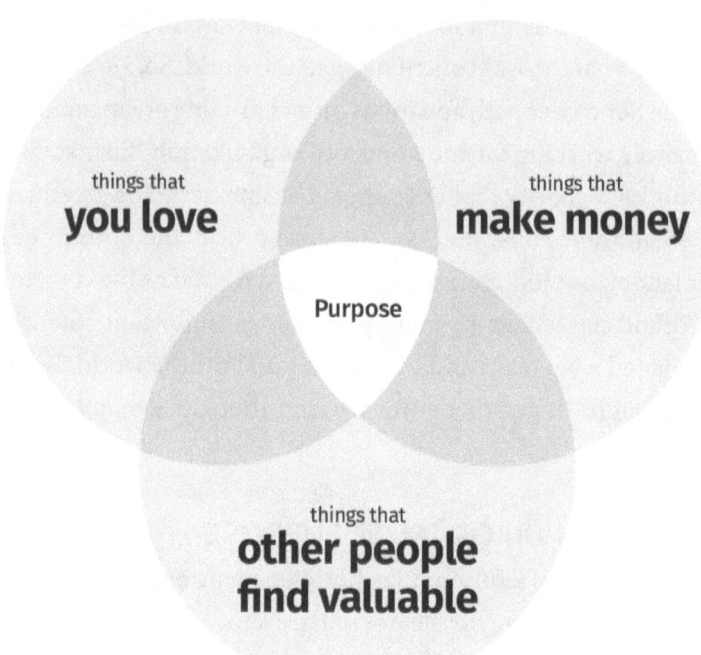

Figure 3—Helen's Venn diagram of Purpose

For many people, "making money" is the priority, which makes complete sense. If you're not making enough money to get by, it can matter much less if you love what you do or if you're contributing to society in a meaningful way. Remember Isabel's question to Margot Dufresne: "What if you have to follow your heart *and* you gotta pay your rent?"

My father always used to recite a similar though more politely phrased maxim, "Do what you love, and the money will follow." In retrospect, I think he worried about my ability to make a living wage after I decided not to become a doctor or a lawyer, chose to pursue a dead-end English degree, and then got fired from my first job. Sadly, he died only a year later and never got to see that I followed his advice and had a successful career.

Doing what you love while making money is good, but does it end there? Helen's Venn diagram says it's not enough. The "things that other people find valuable" circle initially confuses people. Doesn't anything that makes you money provide value to somebody else? Perhaps, but I think what Helen meant was more about contributing to society in a meaningful way. She understood the gratifying effect of providing value by doing nonprofit work and, as a professional artist, bringing people joy with her art. Unsurprisingly, many studies show that altruism, in general, increases happiness,[10] health,[11] and even lifespan.[12] But of course, not all vocations are altruistic, let alone provide significant value to others. For example, many transactional jobs, where lots of money can be made, do not contribute to society in a meaningful way—think stockbroker, crypto investor, or currency trader. Nothing against the people who focus their time on these activities, but it's worth considering who really benefits from their work and how. Are the people who work those jobs receiving much intrinsic satisfaction from helping others, or are they just making more money for themselves and others?

The true fulfillment of one's purpose will only come when a job satisfies all three circles—the green intersection of Helen's Venn diagram. During my career, I was fortunate enough to design and build products that provided value to hundreds of millions of people; I loved doing the work, and it paid the bills. I was lucky in part because I was a member of extremely talented teams that were able to execute well on a few great ideas at the right time. Would I have considered my career successful if I were paid well to work on products that didn't affect so many people in such a positive way? Career-wise, family-wise, perhaps, but I wouldn't have felt the intrinsic gratification of knowing how people found value in what I worked on.

• • •

If you can find your purpose, there's surprisingly strong evidence that it is not only fulfilling but healthy for you. In a 2014 study of over 7,000 people aged fifty and older, University of Michigan researcher Eric Kim and his associates found that having a purpose correlates with increased preventive health-care activities.[13] After adjusting for sociodemographic factors, a subject's self-reported purpose score correlated positively to the likelihood of obtaining a cholesterol test or colonoscopy. In addition, women in the study with higher purpose scores were more likely to receive a mammogram or Pap smear, and men were more likely to receive a prostate exam. Given the results of that study, it probably isn't surprising that all-cause mortality rates improve for people with a purpose.

Canadian researcher Patrick Hill and his associate Nicholas Turiano at the University of Rochester conducted a fourteen-year study that found purposeful individuals lived longer than those without a purpose, even when controlling for other markers of psychological well-being.[14] In addition, the longevity benefits do not depend on the participants' age or whether they retired. In other words, having a purpose appears to widely buffer against mortality risk across the adult years.

• • •

Working at the nonprofit only filled in two of those three circles for Helen. She made a healthy living, and of course, working at a nonprofit satisfied that feeling of providing value for others. She noted, "Lots of us have been in jobs that we hate, and we feel like we're just selling our soul . . . but I wasn't in that situation. I was in quite a nice, comfortable situation." Yet it wasn't truly what she loved to do. She was missing the "things you love" circle and, therefore, hadn't found her true purpose.

Well into her career, at twenty-nine, Helen signed up for an art class. She hadn't created any art for twelve years. Helen felt "it was a childish pursuit that I packed away somehow." What spawned the idea of signing up for an art class wasn't any fantasy of a career change. It was that she had recently broken up with her boyfriend, had two weeks of vacation time, and needed something to fill the void of her lost relationship. So, she signed up for a two-week summer session at the prestigious Slade School of Fine Art in London. The school offers fun sessions to the general public, but its more serious side includes bachelor's, master's, and PhD degrees in various forms of fine art. The Slade School has produced scores of famous alumni dating back to the late nineteenth century. A couple of the more recent ones include sculptor Anish Kapoor, who created Cloud Gate (a.k.a. "the Bean"), the huge mirrored stainless-steel sculpture in Chicago's Millennium Park, and pop artist Peter Blake, maybe most famous for the *Sgt. Pepper's Lonely Hearts Club Band* album cover art.

For two weeks, Helen showed up at Slade every day from 9 a.m. to 5 p.m., and quickly, the glimmer that had been flickering inside her all along started glowing brighter. "It felt like a homecoming.... I just loved it.... It felt very positive, very expansive." And that was her reintroduction to art. It was just a hobby, a *serious* hobby. After the two-week course, she spent significant time making art at home while continuing to work. Funny enough, she didn't feel the quality of her work during that period was very good—calling it "rubbish art" at one point. After the twelve-year hiatus, Helen loved creating art, but she arguably wasn't that good at it yet.

For the next few years, Helen aggressively pursued art as a hobby "with loads of classes and loads of learning and loads of reading and loads of just really immersing myself in it." She did all this with a full-time job and still had no intention of becoming a self-supporting artist. "There were quite a few years where it all felt a bit hard, but I knew that I enjoyed it and got a lot of pleasure out of it, and it felt motivating and exciting to me."

After three years, Helen felt the only way to continue this pursuit was to get an art degree. So, at thirty-two, she applied to another prestigious London art school, Central Saint Martin. The admissions process hinges on a single interview where the applicant presents their portfolio to a panel of faculty and describes their process, the meaning behind the work, and how it might fit in the context of today's world. "I was so nervous. I felt like my whole future life was dependent on this interview. And I really just fluffed it up. I couldn't talk eloquently about my work."

The feedback from her interview matched Helen's perception: "Unable to talk about her work with any clarity." Helen was rejected from Central Saint Martin, and for a short while, she admitted defeat. She took out of this experience that "The people who make decisions about these things have decided that *I'm not good enough*."

At thirty-two, Helen gave up creating art again.

Helen had firmly found her glimmer, but on her journey to find her purpose, her "things you love" circle was still empty because she completely stopped doing art at that point. We'll see how she triumphed over this crushing experience soon, but first, let's touch on the third camp of people looking for their glimmer—those for whom someone else decides what your glimmer is.

YOUR PARENT'S GLIMMER IS NOT YOURS

Jason Lee is an unassuming, soft-spoken twenty-six-year-old. He's confident and charismatic, too, but does not come across as the kind of person who runs a real estate brokerage firm that transacted over $300M in assets in less than four years. Commercial real estate is the bastion of old-school gray hairs (or maybe dyed black hairs). By contrast, Jason runs a team of twenty-somethings who are shaking up the business of buying and selling multifamily apartment complexes in San Diego County. Jason did not get this opportunity handed to him either. He came from humble beginnings in the small town of Clayton, California. For parts of Jason's childhood, his mother had to clean houses to make ends meet.

But Jason's parents had high expectations of him. With only the best intentions, they controlled his every move—like *every* move, from every morsel he ate to his limited friend options to his strict bedtime ritual. This tight parental control continued until Jason was about fifteen, when he rebelled enough to unlock a few freedoms. While they still monitored him carefully, Jason was allowed to "hang out with friends" on a time-limited basis. Being social in general and particularly part of a cohesive group was something that Jason craved and would later become an important contributor to his success. Some of that standard rebellious teenage behavior coincided with Jason becoming more serious about athletics.

As a scrawny freshman, Jason mostly rode the bench for both the football and rugby teams at Clayton Valley Charter High School. While he was admittedly terrible at football his freshman year, he absolutely loved it. He loved the camaraderie, the strategy, and the competitiveness. His love of the game motivated him to work hard that summer—bulking up, gaining speed, and improving his "mental toughness." None of this was easy, of course, but he worked through it simply because he liked football. Not surprisingly, multiple studies show that it's easier to learn new skills or attain new knowledge in areas in which you're interested.[15] [16] The reciprocal is also true: it's much harder to learn subjects that you hate. Jason was rewarded for his hard work by earning a starting position on the football team as a sophomore. By his senior year, Jason was named captain of the rugby team and a leader on the football team, which went 13-2 that year and 5-0 in their division. It was through athletics that Jason realized focus and hard work could make a huge difference.

When it came to academics, Jason was a good student, getting mostly As and a few Bs, but he wasn't passionate about any particular subject. "All I cared about was athletics." When it came to deciding what he would do with this life, Jason didn't have a strong opinion, so he "just picked [what] my parents were telling me." Jason's parents dreamed that he would be a successful physician one day. With high hopes, they desperately wanted him to attend one of the more prestigious University of California schools like Berkeley or UCLA. But Jason didn't get into any of the UC schools and was destined to head south to his last choice, San Diego State University.

While a solid academic school with an underrated[17] premed program, San Diego State was not the place Jason's parents dreamed of for their son. At the time, everyone was a little disappointed. Later, Jason said that going to San Diego State was "probably the best thing that's ever happened to me." This was partly due to San Diego being 500 miles away from his parents in Clayton—affording him even more freedom. It also brought him to a growing, densely populated area rich in real estate transactions.

San Diego State's premed curriculum required a year of general chemistry, organic chemistry, and various biology, physics, and biochemistry coursework. But it was the chemistry that Jason absolutely hated. He couldn't stand the subject, and with each class, each lab, each midterm, his hatred grew. He performed well in these classes, but he had to put in a ton of work to get these grades—up to twenty hours a week studying just chemistry because he felt he wasn't a natural at it. Deep in those hours in the library, Jason thought, *Why the hell am I wasting all this time on a stupid subject that I'll never use in real life when I could be learning something [useful]?* When he ran full force into the wall of organic chemistry, Jason was at his breaking point.

GLIMMER EPIPHANY

In the sweeping study *Life Crafting as a Way to Find Purpose and Meaning in Life*,[18] researchers found consistent evidence that pursuing goals prescribed by others rather than self-set goals is associated with reduced motivation, well-being, and life satisfaction. Up until this point, Jason had been pursuing the physician goal prescribed by his parents and was proving this point. After sweating through the organic chemistry final at the end of his first semester junior year, Jason couldn't imagine continuing down this path. He didn't have any idea what he wanted to do, but he simply could not keep battling chemistry. As it was winter break, Jason and his roommates decided to let off some steam by going to a concert featuring the upbeat, melodic music of Louis the Child. They agreed the night before, they were all going to the show on magic mushrooms.

As the electronic beats flowed, deep into his mushroom trip, something struck Jason hard: "That's when I fully made the decision that I was gonna quit the path my parents set me on. [That's when I realized] how much they were holding me back, and I had to do something way bigger in life." According to Jason, "out of thin air," the two concepts of becoming a real estate mogul or doing something important in finance came to him. The day after the concert, he joined the real estate and finance clubs and quickly realized that real estate was far more interesting.

The story of how Jason went from being in the college real estate club to running a multimillion-dollar business in less than five years continues in the "Get Help" chapter. While I wouldn't recommend hallucinogens to help make life decisions, I asked every one of my subjects if they had some kind of epiphany or "aha moment" when they knew they had found the right path. Every single one of them did. For Martha, it was that moment she looked into that boy's eyes and realized that she had to tell her immigrant story to empower others who came after her. For Isabel, it was the moment she realized how quickly she picked up engineering concepts relative to her flight school classmate. And for Helen, it was an even stranger story than Jason's.

WHO'S SHOUTING AT ME?

After Helen's rejection from art school, she nursed her bruised ego for a few months, but she couldn't get the art bug out of her system. Over the next nine years, art became an intense hobby with her cramming night art classes and all-day Saturday sessions in between her day job at the nonprofit. She still liked her job and knew she was doing important work there. At thirty-nine, Helen felt her path was set, balancing her professional life with her hobby.

Then, one day, Helen had to catch a 6 a.m. train to central London for a business meeting. Still a bit sleepy-eyed while waiting on the platform, she noticed someone shouting inappropriately loudly. She couldn't understand it at first, but focusing in, she heard something like, "You're on the wrong path and need to become an artist."

Recounting the story, Helen said, "It took me a moment to [realize], oh my God, there's no one here. *I'm shouting at me.* I'm slightly embarrassed to even talk about it because hearing voices is not cool. But that's how it felt—like someone was shouting at me." Helen self-diagnosed that it must have been her subconscious that knew something her conscious self wasn't acknowledging—being an artist was her true purpose.

"It sounds bananas to even say it out loud, to be honest . . . [but] it was such a powerful experience. I really took note of it. It felt like an important pivot point that I [could] not ignore."

From that moment forward, Helen completely reengineered her life to dedicate it to her art. The next week, she quit her job. She had saved up about six months' worth of living expenses, and this financial cushion gave her a clear timeline to work through how she could make enough money to pay for her life. At that point, Helen had absolutely no idea how to become a self-supporting artist. She had never sold a piece or monetized her work in any way—she hadn't even looked into it. Given the persistent "starving artist" stereotype, it's clear that making a living as an artist is not easy. A 2018 ArtNet study[19] of over 1,000 artists reported that only about 10 percent can live solely on proceeds from their art—and this study is self-reported, possibly biased toward people who might do well.

We'll see how she worked through the Bumpy Part of becoming a self-supporting artist later, but now that Helen had found her purpose, she was both scared and excited to jump on this new learning curve.

BE OPEN TO YOUR PURPOSE

One commonality among most of the subjects of this book is that they did not find their purpose through the standard channels of the primary, secondary, or university education system. Unfortunately, Western educational systems seem to focus on churning out students who pass standardized tests with a baseline of knowledge that, at best, would have helped students succeed in the 1990s. This system isn't designed to help students find their purpose unless it centers on academics itself. A few of the people in this book, including me, found their purpose at work, but only by being exposed to a different function than their own.

At twenty-five, I landed a job at Microsoft as a systems engineer within the enterprise sales team. At that time, there were only nineteen systems engineers covering the entire country, and we had to support everything from the early versions of Microsoft Word and Excel to programming languages like Fortran and Visual Basic. Whenever a new version of a product was released, someone from headquarters came to our sales office to hype us up about the new features.

One day, the Microsoft Word product manager came to tell us about the latest version of her product. She was incredibly sharp, presented the material thoughtfully, and was absolutely beautiful. I instantly had a crush on her and, at the same time, wanted her job. My understanding of how software products were built was a bit fuzzy until that point. I had assumed the software engineers not only coded the software but also made all the other decisions about how the software would work and appear to the consumer. Of course, it's much more complex than that—many designers, businesspeople, and other technical personnel are involved in producing a complex product like Microsoft Word.

I learned from that visit that the product manager oversees the whole thing. She managed which features would go in the next version of Microsoft Word, how those features were incorporated into the product, and how they'd be exposed to the consumer—its user interface.

As a systems engineer, my work only affected, at most, a few hundred people at a time. Being the decision-maker on a product that made millions of people more productive and sometimes even happy would be much more fulfilling. Plus, I could "fix" all the annoying things I hated about Microsoft products. I followed up with the product manager, Melinda French, and asked her how she got the job.

She said Microsoft recruited her out of Duke's Fuqua MBA program. As I probed the organization more, it seemed that pretty much every product manager at Microsoft had an MBA from a top business school. At that moment, I decided I was going to get an MBA to fulfill my newly found purpose—to be a product manager for a technology product.

As for my fleeting crush on Melinda, later, it became clear that another Microsoft employee had a crush on her too: Bill Gates. If you didn't recognize her name, Melinda French married Bill Gates in 1994, spent twenty-four years as the cochair of the Bill & Melinda Gates Foundation, and, as of this writing, is working on a $250 million initiative focused on improving the mental and physical health of women and girls globally.

That chance meeting with Melinda sparked the career pivot that would propel my career for the next thirty years. Whether you stumble across your purpose as Isabel and I did, or it slaps you in the face as it did with Jason and Helen, you owe it to yourself to be open to it. *And* to take action. Of course, there are many counterfactual cases where taking action may lead to painful failure (see Helen's initial attempt applying to art school), but if you don't take action, one thing is certain: nothing will change. As soon as Isabel had the realization that she may have an innate engineering talent, she started talking to professors at the University of Houston. When Jason had his real estate epiphany, he joined the real estate club and changed his major to communications to graduate as fast as he could. And soon after Melinda told me about her recruitment from Duke, I started studying for the GMAT in preparation for applying to MBA programs.

The rest of the book assumes you've found your glimmer and possibly evolved it to a purpose. Either way, it's time to start learning "shortcuts" to get you across the Bumpy Part of the learning curve.

PRACTICAL GUIDE/SUMMARY

- Finding your "glimmer" (a strong feeling that draws you to a subject area or activity) is the first step toward discovering your purpose in life.

- Look for the intersection of these when finding your purpose: things you love, things that make money, and things that other people find valuable.

- If you have a glimmer buried inside you, find ways to pursue it as a hobby while still paying the bills with your main career. Give it time to evolve into a purpose.

- Don't ignore "aha moments" or epiphanies where your purpose becomes clear to you. This could come from meeting someone inspirational, having a life experience, or just a strong gut feeling.

- Be willing to take action as soon as you sense your purpose. Don't overthink it or wait for the perfect circumstances.

- Don't let setbacks deter you from pursuing your purpose. See them as part of the learning process—the Bumpy Part of the curve.

- The traditional education system may not lead you directly to your purpose. Be open to finding it through work experiences, hobbies, or unexpected life events.

For more extensive guidance and exercises to help you find your glimmer or purpose, check out the *Outsmart the Learning Curve Workbook* at https://www.outsmartbook.com/workbook or use the QR code below.

CHAPTER 2
OPENNESS

You can observe a lot by just watching.

—Yogi Berra

PERHAPS THE MOST surprising finding for me in researching this book was that an attitude of openness was central to the success of every one of the subjects I covered. You already saw evidence of openness leading people to their purpose with Isabel, her satisficer strategy of exploring different vocations, from game marketer to web hosting marketer, and being remarkably open to her destiny as an aerospace engineer. And both Helen and Jason had to be open to their subconscious selves telling them they were pursuing the wrong purpose. More closed-minded people might suppress or ignore those internal messages, but thankfully, neither Helen nor Jason did.

In psychology, the term openness is one of the "Big Five" personality traits[20]—a taxonomy that describes human personalities based on these five attributes: openness, conscientiousness, extraversion, agreeableness, and neuroticism (sometimes abbreviated OCEAN). The Big Five traits have been studied intensely since the 1980s, with academics having researched almost every imaginable correlation between these traits and other human attributes such as gender, culture, birth order, academic achievement, work performance, and more. People high in openness (sometimes referred to as "openness to experience") tend to try new things, prefer variety and diversity, and be more curious about their environment.

Those attributes align well with the people profiled in this book who made dramatic transformations or overcame significant obstacles. As we'll see later, increased openness can also lead people to make incremental changes or simply lead to a more fulfilling life. Most importantly, people have the ability to *change* their level of openness. Before we dive deeper into the rich research around openness, let's continue Isabel's story as an illustration of how her openness personality trait aided her journey through the Bumpy Part of her ride to becoming an aerospace engineer.

ISABEL UPROOTS HER LIFE IN A CRAZY WAY

Soon after Isabel realized she may have some innate engineering talent, she drove the twenty-five minutes from her day job at HostGator to the University of Houston's Engineering Department to see if she could find someone to talk to.

"I just walked around and found some professors and was like, all right, here's my story. 'I'm a marketing manager with a pilot's license. I'm thinking about trying engineering. What do you think?' And literally all of them, one after the other, three in a row who did not know each other independently, were like, yeah, that's a crazy idea. I think they all said, 'How old are you?' And then when I told them, they were like, yeah, that's a crazy idea."

Thirty-six-year-old Isabel drove back to her office in silence and sank into her cubicle chair. While she was a bit dejected, at least she had confirmation that it was time to put this engineering school idea to bed. Yet Isabel couldn't put it to bed. She found herself drawing schematics of fuel systems at work while she should have been handling her regular marketing responsibilities. She couldn't stop thinking about aerospace engineering.

After about a week, she did a little more research and realized that each of the three professors she spoke to were in the University of Houston's Space Architecture program, not the Aerospace Engineering Department. So Isabel decided to give it one more try by visiting the dean of the Aerospace Engineering Department. She arrived during his standard office hours and awkwardly waited in line with a bunch of college kids for over an hour. When it was finally her turn, the dean said, "How can I help you?" Isabel responded with her story about being a marketing manager with a pilot's license. Would it be crazy to go for a master's in aerospace engineering? "And then I just held my breath and waited for 'this is a stupid idea.'" Instead, the dean said, "Of course you can do it." And Isabel said, "That's what I've been thinking!"

• • •

The academic research on the openness trait has uncovered compelling evidence that people high on the openness scale are likely to have increased life satisfaction,[21] higher educational attainment,[22] improved physical and mental functioning in older adults,[23] and even a longer life.[24] At a minimum, Isabel's story is illustrative of the educational attainment finding. In the face of rejection from three different college professors, she was still open enough, curious enough to find a fourth person. I suspect if the dean of the Aerospace Engineering Department had said "no," Isabel would have continued to seek out professors elsewhere until she heard a yes. Could you call this behavior resilience? Yes, and there's an upcoming chapter dedicated to that, but it's especially hard to be resilient in the face of rejection when you're not *very* open to the idea in the first place.

OPENNESS DOESN'T MEAN TAKING INSANE RISKS

After the dean told Isabel that she could earn a master's in aerospace engineering, the next question was how could she possibly pull this off? As a marketing professional in the digital era, a central aspect of Isabel's day job was to set up experiments, in marketing-speak A/B tests, to figure out which ad or marketing message performed best under what circumstances. Digital marketers often perform these A/B tests on smaller audiences before spending the big bucks on the winning ad or message. Doing this kind of A/B testing on smaller audiences reduces the risk of spending millions on an ineffective ad campaign, broadly deploying a terrible feature, or providing a new service no one wants.

Isabel wanted to apply similar testing principles before making her risky career move. So she asked the dean, "Is there any way I can test this before I uproot my life and quit my job?" He thought about it for a minute and suggested that if she could get through the rigorous prerequisite calculus coursework, then she could get through the aerospace engineering program.

Isabel was looking at the Bumpy Part of the aerospace engineering macro learning curve and saw quite a long and painful road. While at a high level, it would seem outlandish for a mid-career thirty-six-year-old to start on a master's in a completely different field than she's ever studied, Isabel's strategy was quite clever: mitigate the risk as you go. She wasn't going to "uproot her life in a crazy way" unless she could get some sense of the possibility of success, that is, to test her ability in a low-risk way. The dean obliged and said if she could pass the calculus prerequisites, she could do the work to get a master's degree. So Isabel didn't really have to jump in with both feet, and she wasn't the only person profiled in this book who deployed trying things out in a low-risk way to get through the Bumpy Part of the learning curve.

JEREMY COULDN'T FIGURE OUT KINDERGARTEN

After taking a college childhood education course that included an inner-city Philadelphia field teaching element, energetic Jeremy Schifeling decided to dedicate his life to education. He wanted to be lauded like Jaime Escalante, the high school teacher portrayed in *Stand and Deliver*, who shocked the world when 100 percent of his East Los Angeles AP calculus students passed the exam. He wanted to be revered like Robin Williams's character in *Dead Poets Society*, who became an inspiration and hero to his students. Jeremy wanted to be that fun teacher who lifted everyone up and made learning cool.

Jeremy started his teaching career as a substitute for an inner-city Philadelphia school district. Of course, substitute teaching isn't the greatest gig for most people. If not handled well, the job often spirals into a glorified babysitter. After sampling a variety of grades through his substitute teaching experience, Jeremy decided fifth grade would be his ideal age to teach because it was a "good balance between kids still being interested and hungry to learn but not being babies." Several months into his grueling substitute teaching role, the principal called and asked Jeremy if he wanted his own classroom. "That sounds great!" said Jeremy. But there was a catch: all the principal could offer was a kindergarten class. Jeremy wasn't thrilled. He didn't want to continue being mostly a babysitter. The principal sensed Jeremy's hesitancy and offered, "If you can teach kindergarten, you can teach anything." That challenge convinced Jeremy to take the kindergarten job.

With a full-time classroom, Jeremy was able to implement many of his fun-loving, gamified teaching ideas that he'd been dreaming up. He created a kindergarten *Jeopardy* game. He built various sophisticated reward systems. He let his personality come through in everything he did. The only problem was that none of it worked. He tried every approach he could think of to get these kids to engage in learning, but the rambunctious five-year-olds did not cooperate.

After months of trying every "nice guy" methodology he could think of, Jeremy resorted to the very approach he did not want to use—to be more disciplined and controlled but not necessarily loved. Instead of a free-flowing classroom that often turned into chaos, in desperation, Jeremy decided to try a technique he saw in movies about Harvard Law School called the Socratic method. He essentially started cold calling on the five-year-olds like a stern law professor. One person talks at a time and only when called upon. To his shock, this technique worked. "Things really clicked . . . when I gave up on the nice guy teacher act and said I'm gonna give the kids absolutely one-hundred-percent confidence about what to expect." According to Jeremy, the kids loved the new methodology too.

Jeremy surmised that his students thrived under the new technique because many of these children found themselves enmeshed in chaotic lives outside of the classroom. The kindergartners thrived on the structure inside the classroom because they often had too little of it outside the classroom. The students knew exactly how every day would operate, and that gave them a foundation from which to learn.

BE OPEN TO SURPRISING RESULTS OF A/B TESTS

Jeremy was shocked this last-ditch effort to incorporate more structure into the classroom was the technique that worked. His use of trial and error is a rudimentary form of A/B testing that Isabel also used. Instead of continuing down a path that didn't work, Jeremy systematically tried new techniques and used measurements to compare one method versus another.

Jeremy's story contains two valuable lessons. First, while thought experiments are nice, they don't prove anything. To validate if an approach, technique, or method is going to work—even one about self-improvement—it must be done in the real world. Jeremy had pored over all these creative ideas about how to engage children in the classroom. When reading about them or developing them at home, they sounded like they were certain to work. In the real world, as shown by his pseudo-A/B tests, none of these brilliant ideas engaged the kindergarteners.

The second lesson is that you need to be open to approaches that might sound crazy or have a low probability of working. As

Jeremy noted, these crazy ideas are often "where the gold is"—the ideas, approaches, and concepts that other people haven't tried or considered but then disregarded because "that'll never work." By A/B testing ideas in the real world, you can make surprising discoveries and build that learning into your "muscle memory," as Jeremy puts it: "For me, I baked two things into my muscle memory. I baked what worked eventually, which was great, but I also had the haunting memory of what didn't work."

You may have noticed that I referred to Isabel's and Jeremy's techniques as "pseudo" A/B testing. While their techniques were hugely useful and valid to help them with life decisions, real A/B testing, when possible, is even more likely to yield confidence-building results. Real A/B testing involves hundreds or thousands of test samples and ideally needs to hold everything constant except the variable you're testing. Companies like Google and Facebook use this testing methodology constantly to optimize decisions like what text on a button is the most effective for various situations ("Learn More" vs. "Get Started" vs. "Shop Now").

Of course, in the case of Isabel's and Jeremy's tests, it was impossible to get hundreds of samples or hold all other variables constant. While running a test with fewer samples and/or sequentially can help guide you in the right direction and mitigate risks, if you can run a real A/B experiment to make a decision, you should. Yes, deep-pocketed brands like Google and Facebook constantly A/B test every new feature, but you can do real A/B on a smaller scale for not much money.

For example, I was really struggling with the name of this book. Some people told me they loved *Outsmart the Learning Curve*, but others were really excited about a riskier, possibly more eye-catching name: *But I Suck At...* Others thought that a shorter, more mysterious title would be more effective, like *Jumping Curves*. After taking in as much feedback as possible and bouncing it around in my head for a few months, the right decision wasn't clear to me.

I felt like I needed more real data than asking a few friends and even fewer experts for their opinions. So, I decided to A/B test the book title options to give me confidence in the decision and possibly learn more. Over my career in marketing, I often asked employees or other insiders to predict the results of the A/B tests *before* we ran them. Invariably, many people would be extremely confident in their predictions and wondered why we were even testing at all, given how "obvious" the winner would be. But like Jeremy found out with his kindergartners, results of tests are often surprising and engender learning you couldn't have imagined—and that's exactly what happened with this book title.

First, here's the formula I used to set up a real A/B test for less than $200. To start, I used one of many free or cheap, no-code web editing tools to create three identical landing pages (simple web pages that contain relevant information people will see after clicking on an ad). The only difference between the three landing pages was the title of the book. Many no-code web editing tools allow you to create and host these landing pages with little more technical skill than required to use a word processor. Some modern tools even use AI to generate a landing page based on a short description. Next, I opened a Google Ads account and created three different ad campaigns pointing to the three different landing pages. Again, the only difference between the three campaigns was the title of the book. Unlike the no-code web creation tools, I would be remiss if I didn't mention that, as of this writing, the Google Ads interface can be complicated and confusing, even for someone who's familiar with the concepts like me.

After a frustrating ride on the Bumpy Part of the Google Ads admin learning curve, I started spending $20/day testing all three title options at the same time. Over the week, I ended up spending $145 to get over 36,000 impressions (roughly the number of times the ad was seen) and 362 clicks on one of these ads. I stopped the test because 1) generally, after about 300–400 samples with larger populations, the results will be statistically significant*—that is, you can be pretty confident that the test results reflect what would happen every time you test it—and 2) the results were so heavily weighted to the winner. It's not just that *Outsmart the Learning Curve* had more clicks (and performed better on a deeper interest indicator of entering an email to find out book availability), but the new and surprising information is that I had to fight Google's "policy" systems on *But I Suck At...* every step of the way. First, Google limited the *But I Suck At...* ad's viewability because of the use of ellipses, which apparently aren't allowed. When I removed them, Google's systems claimed my text was "confusing," which I have to agree with, especially without the ellipsis. Finally, Google's automated system didn't seem to like the word *Suck* either. I successfully appealed that decision, but that version just didn't perform as well as *Outsmart the Learning Curve.*

Before the test, my poll predicted *But I Suck At...* would win this A/B test—it's a catchy title containing a titillating word that might generate curiosity clicks. I predicted it would do best on the measure of clicks but possibly worse on the deeper metric of entering an email address. I was completely wrong. I didn't anticipate the policy problems that could have followed this title through every step of the publishing process. How would I have known that unless I tested it? The A/B testing made my decision easy. The bottom line is this: be open to the surprising results of A/B tests no matter how you conduct them.

USING PURPOSE AS A MOTIVATOR

Isabel had finally found the macro learning curve she was supposed to be on: aerospace engineering. But she quickly found herself on the

---

* Even though I couched this in several ways, stat heads will note that 300–400 samples is not always the right number of samples for statistical significance. And they're right! If you'd like to go a little deeper on this without learning formulas, this site does a nice job: https://tools4dev.org/resources/how-to-choose-a-sample-size/.

Bumpy Part of the learning curve, which was composed of a bunch of smaller proficiency curves she had to climb. First, she had to take a placement test to even get into calculus. The prerequisites required her to learn or relearn all the basics from algebra to geometry to trigonometry to precalculus. Just working through all the textbooks and problem sets took her six months "at night, on vacation, on weekends, at lunch—all day, every day." In the end, she didn't feel comfortable with all the material, so she hired a tutor for some of the more esoteric topics. Surprising herself, she passed the placement test in October 2014, and by January 2015, she was enrolled in calculus at night school while continuing to work for HostGator during the day.

Isabel spent six months studying tedious math. Of course, her passion was not mathematics, yet she persisted through some Bumpy Parts of the learning curve. In other aspects of her career, Isabel didn't always follow through as diligently as she did with those prerequisites. She worked hard on the items she cared about—the tasks she felt would make a big difference. And if she didn't think a task would move the needle, sometimes she wouldn't follow through or would let it fall through the cracks (which isn't always a bad idea). Yet on the calculus prerequisites and the rigorous math and physics class that followed, Isabel didn't let anything fall through the cracks and, in fact, approached these stepping-stone classes with deep determination.

How do you muster this level of determination—that is, fight through mundane or difficult tasks to get to your purpose? Before she published her bestselling book, *Grit*, Angela Duckworth and several other researchers published a meta-study (a study of studies) called *Boring but Important: A Self-Transcendent Purpose for Learning Fosters Academic Self-Regulation.*[25] The researchers defined "self-transcendent purpose" much the way we define purpose in this book: a purpose that is driven by a combination of self-benefit and having some effect or connection to the world beyond the self. The findings in this research suggest that if a person is motivated by a self-transcendent purpose, they are more likely to persist through boring, arduous, or deep material when studying as compared to a person without a self-transcendent purpose. While the specific studies in the meta-analysis looked at high school and college students, I suspect it's safe to extrapolate these results to anyone who has found a purpose. It's much easier to work through the Bumpy Part of a learning curve if you're excited about the rewards at the end of that curve. Isabel's goal of becoming an aerospace engineer propelled her through the tedium of those prerequisites. But what motivated her to get through the even more rigorous material of the aerospace engineering master's degree itself was the self-transcendental purpose of helping humankind explore the cosmos.

STUMBLING ON DESTINY

Out of general interest in aerospace engineering, Isabel was curious to visit the Space Center Houston science museum. But she couldn't find the address online. "So I started doing all these different types of searches, and this unpaid Lockheed Martin internship for what I think is probably meant for high school students popped up," she said. Isabel took a few minutes to apply online, thinking, *They can't turn down an old fart like me*, and she forgot about it. Several months later, Lockheed Martin's chief of the Aeronautics Projects office emailed asking if Isabel would like to come help with a flight readiness review program. It was all volunteer, and Lockheed needed at least one day a week. Isabel already had a full-time job and was still attending night school, taking calculus and physics classes. So, she asked her boss at HostGator if she could work four days a week and take a commensurate pay cut. Her manager generously granted the request, and now Isabel was headed to Lockheed every Friday and started learning how this giant, bureaucratic, but amazingly accomplished organization worked. Lockheed Martin's vision of "advancing scientific discovery" exposed Isabel to a higher-level purpose that would refine her own vision and goals for the rest of her career.

This wasn't the first time Isabel used volunteering to move across the Bumpy Part of the learning curve. Remember, Isabel agreed to do a bunch of work for Debra Rossini's game company for free just so she could get her foot in the door of the game industry. As it turns out, doing something for free is a great way to take pressure off the learning process. Many studies provide evidence that learning under pressure can distract,[26] negatively impact information integration,[27] and hamper memory retrieval.[28]

By doing these tasks for free, Isabel took a lot of pressure off her learning environment. If she couldn't complete that first task for Debra Rossini of updating the Flash website, she would have likely just moved on to the next thing—no hard feelings, no guilt, and frankly, little if any fear of failure. The "Confidence" chapter explores several other techniques for how a self-doubting person can become more confident, but one of those tools is to reduce the risk of the learning task by volunteering. By being open to doing jobs for free, Isabel reduced the risk of her failing and the risk of people adversely judging her performance on the task.

The value of doing something for free or volunteering seems lost on many today. Of course, lots of people volunteer their time for charities and the like to contribute to society and feel good about themselves, but I rarely hear stories about people like Isabel, who offer free services in exchange for learning. It wasn't like she had a lot of money or time. But she knew what she wanted and used the exchange of free or low-cost labor to gain skills or prestigious opportunities.

After she got through enough calculus classes to satisfy the dean of the Aeronautics Engineering Department, he helped her pick the necessary aerospace engineering classes with the right timing so she could get her master's as quickly as possible. Around the time she started her master's degree, Lockheed converted her to a full-time employee doing project management work, so she quit her job at HostGator. Isabel still had two years of schooling and a bit of bureaucratic turmoil to get through to become an aerospace engineer, but quitting HostGator meant she officially left her marketing career behind.

The title of this section, "Stumbling on Destiny," describes the haphazard way Isabel fell into her aerospace career—searching for a museum address and finding an internship application meant for high school students. Yet, instead of being described as haphazard or stumbling, Isabel's approach is better described as "openness." In fact, several of the other subjects of this book used terms like "stumbled forward" to describe their journeys, as if they lucked into opportunities. But like Isabel, each kept their eyes and options open and moved forward when an interesting possibility presented itself. Stumbling forward may be a self-deprecating way to describe openness, but it also introduces the idea that perhaps you can make your own luck.

MAKE YOUR OWN LUCK

British psychology professor Richard Wiseman has studied luck for over twenty years. His book *The Luck Factor*[29] asserts that luck is a state of mind versus some mystical ability to transform misfortune into success. His perspective raises the question, "Can you make your own luck?" According to Wiseman, you can. Wiseman and his students surveyed over 700 people, simply asking participants if they considered themselves lucky, unlucky, or neutral. Then he followed up with a series of tests:

- Asking participants to predict how well they would do at a card guessing game.

- Presenting two metal puzzles, only one of which was solvable. Based on a coin toss, they were handed one of the two puzzles and asked if they got the solvable or unsolvable one.

- Asking them to count the number of photos in a newspaper.

- To a statistically significant degree, *lucky and unlucky people approached the tasks in completely opposite ways.* How could that be? The lucky people had a different approach to life than the unlucky ones.

THREE PILLARS TO MAKE YOUR OWN LUCK

OPTIMISM

When asked to predict how well they would do at a game of guessing black or red playing cards, unlucky people generally went with the odds (fifty-fifty), but lucky people consistently predicted that they would do *better* than the odds. Statistically, the unlucky people were correct—on average, everyone in the study guessed about half the cards right.

However, the goal was not to see who could guess the most cards correctly but rather to understand the mindset of people who considered themselves lucky. The lucky people felt they had some advantage. They were optimistic that they could beat the odds. As we'll see later, this optimistic mindset leads to many other benefits.

RESILIENCE

On the metal puzzle test, based on a coin toss, each participant was given one of the two puzzles and asked if they got the solvable or unsolvable one. Unbeknownst to the participants, *both* metal puzzles were unsolvable. Yet, 70 percent of the lucky people thought they received the solvable one, while 60 percent of the unlucky people thought they received the unsolvable one.

The lucky people also spent more time diligently trying to solve the puzzle and often had to be asked to stop at a time limit. The self-proclaimed unlucky people spent much less time trying. Unlucky people just gave up on their own, while the lucky people showed more determination in the face of unlikely odds.

OPENNESS

On the counting newspaper photos test, the people who considered themselves unlucky took about two minutes to find the photos, while the lucky people were able to complete the tasks in seconds. The difference? On the second page of the newspaper, there was a giant ad that said, "Stop counting. There are forty-three photos in this newspaper." Lucky people were much more likely to see this shortcut than unlucky people.

Wiseman theorized that those who considered themselves lucky were more likely to keep their eyes open for the shortcut because they exhibited the "openness" personality trait. In a different study, Wiseman gave participants a Big Five personality test and found that those high on the openness scale correlated with those who consider themselves lucky.

Pretty much all the people profiled in this book noted a serendipitous event that changed the course of their lives. They probably wouldn't be in this book if they hadn't acted on those serendipitous moments. For example, before Jeremy's short-lived kindergarten teaching career, he experienced a serendipitous event that had an even more profound impact on his career than his learnings from being a failed kindergarten teacher.

JEREMY MAKES HIS OWN LUCK

Before Jeremy started his one-year teaching stint, in the vein of Helen's Venn diagram of purpose, his ambitious mind was set on doing something that could help more people at a time than a classroom of thirty students. This was around 2004 when a nonprofit called Teach for America was gaining popularity among college graduates and the education community. Teach for America recruited college graduates from top universities to commit to two-year K-12 teaching stints in fifty-two low-income communities. Over the years, Teach for America has recruited over 50,000 teachers who collectively taught more than 5,000,000 students.[30] Jeremy wanted to do something on the scale of Teach for America "to make a dent in the universe," and what better way than by joining that organization? So Jeremy applied for a one-year fellowship to become a member of the recruiting team, and he got the job.

One of the reasons Jeremy found this fellowship attractive was the one-year time limit. This constraint provided optionality—after the fellowship, he could choose to follow his initial dream of teaching, continue working at Teach for America in another role, or perhaps this fellowship or other life experiences could lead him down a completely different path. One aspect of the openness personality trait is being open to the next great career move rather than sticking to a narrow career plan.[31]

The recruiting process at Teach for America was pretty "high touch" at the time, with recruiters flying to universities all over the country, giving presentations, and being on the ground with student candidates. However, the fun travel and social activities were reserved for the more senior people on the recruiting team who were either previous teachers in the program or had been a part of the recruiting team for a while. On the other hand, the recruiting fellows' job involved menial tasks such as scheduling travel or coordinating with university personnel to organize information sessions they would never attend. About forty people were hired in this recruiting fellowship class, and thirty-nine of them were assigned subordinate roles to more senior recruiters to handle the menial stuff. For some reason, Jeremy was singled out for a completely different and far more interesting job.

To that point, Teach for America had been a pretty elitist organization. The founder, Wendy Kopp, graduated from Princeton, started the program there, and subsequently built strong relationships with all the Ivy League schools as well as other top universities. Of course, the most exclusive universities only turn out a tiny fraction of the graduating seniors in any given year. Teach for America was missing out on the vast majority of potential recruits. Jeremy's job was to come up with a program to attract candidates from the hundreds of colleges that Teach for America had not specifically recruited from up until that point.

This well-established nonprofit chose to put a lone fresh college grad in charge of recruiting thousands of students from hundreds of universities to an organization they likely had never heard of. This job would be a gargantuan marketing task for anyone, let alone a twenty-two-year-old with no marketing training. But Jeremy was excited for the challenge and immediately dug right in. The hands-on approach of sending paid Teach for America recruiters to each university to build awareness and encourage applications could not easily scale to hundreds of universities. With a little research, Jeremy realized that not all the Teach for America alumni came from top schools. A few people from nearly every university joined Teach for America in any given year. So, he came up with the idea to create an alumni-based recruiting approach. He reached out to hundreds of these alumni to see if they would go back to their alma mater and present the Teach for America concept to graduating seniors at scheduled information sessions. Jeremy spent six months coming up with this program, recruiting the alumni, coordinating the travel and each info session that would happen on campus, and doing the local marketing at each university so people would show up at the info session. And guess what happened?

"Nothing happened. [The alumni] went back, hung out with some professors, and did an info session with, like, five people in the audience. It was a complete dud."

In fact, the application numbers from Jeremy's target schools went *down* compared to the previous year. Jeremy had hit a serious bump on his Teach for America recruiting learning curve. He had burned the first six months of his fellowship and $100,000 of Teach for America's money for travel and other expenses and had nothing to show for it. Amazingly, Teach for America didn't fire Jeremy or even pull him off the project—instead, they let him try again. Given only two application deadlines per year, he had one more attempt. "I could not afford to fail this time."

Jeremy had no idea what to do for his second and final attempt. He had spent the first six months so focused on his first approach that he hadn't even thought about other ways to solve this problem. Jeremy "was so consumed in [his] own little bubble" that he never looked for other ways to solve the recruiting problem. Being overly focused can get in the way of openness. In fact, being overly focused can get in the way of luck too. Wiseman found that people high on the neuroticism personality trait were less likely to be lucky than those low on that scale. In the context of the Big Five, people high on the neuroticism scale are prone to anxiety and worry and tend to focus on what could go wrong. Whereas people lower in neuroticism are more relaxed and stay attentive to opportunities that others miss. Jeremy needed this initial failure to take him out of his overly focused state and find a new way to solve the problem. "It was only at the end of my rope, when things were looking so bleak, that I bothered to open my eyes."

Jeremy sat next to a second-year fellow named Christian. Christian probably could have helped Jeremy with a lot of tasks along the way. Yet for the first six months of Jeremy's fellowship, he barely said hello to the guy. On the day Jeremy realized he had no idea what to do, when his mindset was more open, he decided to look over his neighbor's shoulder at his computer screen and ask, "What are you doing?" Christian was using Microsoft Excel to organize a small database of his own recruiting targets. Christian went on to describe how Excel's Pivot Tables and the VLOOKUP function helped him manage names, addresses, and other information about a few hundred potential candidates. This blew Jeremy's mind. Note that Jeremy was a double political science and education major who had never been exposed to spreadsheets. Quickly, Jeremy realized that if he could apply the principles that Christian had used on hundreds of names, he could extrapolate the same techniques to hundreds of thousands.

Christian showed him how he could integrate the Excel list of names and contact information with email to completely automate personalized emails based on the student's name, school, clubs, and major. Yes, Jeremy (re)invented email marketing. Now Jeremy "could send out an email that would reach a hundred thousand students in just one hour. Every single email was uniquely personalized and looked like it had been drafted for them based on their major, their clubs, and what they were excited about." Maybe you can sense the excitement in Jeremy's voice from that quote—that's the tone of someone quickly going up the steepest part of the learning curve—and Jeremy's inflection point? A single day chatting with the random guy sitting next to him at work.

While not a new concept in many circles, at Teach for America, email marketing was a revolutionary idea. In place of all the work and expense of setting up in-person meetings, now they could reach hundreds of thousands of students in less time than setting up a single in-person meeting for practically no cost. Jeremy even boosted the value of the campaign by using rudimentary viral marketing techniques such as suggesting people share the email with others who might be interested in Teach for America and creating contests between different college clubs to see who could generate the most applicants. In the end, Jeremy's second attempt at recruiting was a raging success. His college targets generated 30 percent of all the successfully recruited teachers that year and powered a record-breaking 171 percent increase in new teachers overall.

Multiple times in our conversations, Jeremy referred to himself as lucky. He was lucky to get the fellowship with Teach for America, to be assigned a unique responsibility for his fellowship, and to sit next to Christian, who was so helpful. Of course, while there was some luck involved, Richard Wiseman would argue that Jeremy made his own luck by being open to and taking advantage of opportunities that presented themselves.

BE OPEN TO WHAT'S STARING YOU RIGHT IN THE FACE

After his one-year stint as a kindergarten teacher and with the Teach for America email marketing experience under his belt, Jeremy fortified and applied these concepts for the next four years at two different nonprofits that recruited young professionals. At the end of his fourth year, Jeremy didn't feel like he was growing. He wanted to "learn how the other half lives . . . in for-profit Silicon Valley." So he went back to school to get his MBA, and as he was nearing graduation, Jeremy had job offers from Google, Amazon, Microsoft, and LinkedIn. Jeremy chose LinkedIn because they offered him a role centered on education, Jeremy's lifelong passion. Jeremy's job was to use a variety of digital methodologies to recruit students and recent graduates on to LinkedIn's professional social network. Jeremy excelled at his job not through his MBA school but because of his early work at Teach for America—those same learnings spawned by that one day with Christian.

Jeremy only spent two years at LinkedIn and went on to join a much smaller startup in the education technology arena as a vice president. This was an exciting opportunity for Jeremy at first, but after a couple of years, Jeremy realized he wasn't happy with the direction of the company. He felt he had better ideas than the company's founder and CEO. When you live and work in Silicon Valley, you hear about people with their own ideas leaving the safety of a bigger company and starting something independently. The ethos of Silicon Valley is centered on people who bet on themselves, create new companies, and sometimes even invent new categories of products or services. It all sounds so exciting and fun until you try it.

Once Jeremy realized that he couldn't change management's mind about the direction of the company, he abruptly quit his job and started his own company the next day. His new business idea was somewhat autobiographical—because he had gone from being a failed kindergarten teacher to "making it" in Silicon Valley, he felt he could help other people outside Silicon Valley break into the intimidating and mysterious world of technology. His initial target market was the cohort of MBAs who were sick of their consulting, banking, and consumer packaged goods jobs and ready to get into tech. Jeremy came up with a logo, built a website, defined a coaching program, created a curriculum, and, after three months, earned $20 in revenue, which was for coaching a friend. One might argue Jeremy was a bit rash in his decision to quit his job and start a company on an unproven business idea, and that one person might be his wife, who had just given birth to their second child.

In his own words, Jeremy was completely humbled. He'd boasted to his friends and family about how he would become a successful Silicon Valley entrepreneur and how incredible his new venture would be. The reality was that Jeremy made a lot of classic entrepreneurial mistakes, such as spending too much time on his company's logo and website rather than understanding whether anyone would pay for the services he planned to offer. In the same way, Jeremy initially focused on the trappings of being the beloved teacher and only later realized that strategy wasn't going to make for successful students; he also fell into the trappings of being an entrepreneur focusing on the glamorous parts of a startup versus the hard work of understanding customer needs. Given his dire situation at home, Jeremy went back to his MBA alma mater, the University of Michigan Ross School of Business, and "begged them to give me a job" as their tech career coach. Michigan did bring him on, but Jeremy continued pushing his theme of "making it in Silicon Valley" without understanding the needs of his customers, the career center at Michigan, and the graduating second-year students.

The likely reason Michigan hired Jeremy was not because he had a track record helping people find jobs in tech—he didn't. They hired him because he had LinkedIn on his résumé. Jeremy's two years at LinkedIn gave him an inside view into how that social network worked, what was important and not important, how recruiters viewed LinkedIn profiles, and how to optimize those profiles for the highest levels of viewability and interest. While the Michigan students and career services team felt that LinkedIn was an important, albeit mysterious black box, Jeremy wanted to pursue his original idea of tips and tricks for getting into tech. Yet, day in and day out, the career services staff asked Jeremy to share his LinkedIn knowledge: create LinkedIn guides for graduating second-year students, conduct information sessions, and then repeat those sessions to various audiences. To Jeremy, this was all tedious and getting in the way of his real work.

"When I heard it for the fifth or tenth or hundredth time, that's when the light bulb went off. That's the thing, dummy. That's what people want."

Until that moment, Jeremy wasn't open to the idea that his LinkedIn knowledge was incredibly valuable and, because of his inside knowledge, unique to him. So, he went all in on the LinkedIn aspect of his job. Once he finally understood his value to Michigan, he quickly realized that his unique approach could be applied to many universities. Career services organizations inside large universities often have seven-figure budgets with no one who knows the first thing about LinkedIn. Yet, LinkedIn is central to their recruiting process. So Jeremy took the template he created at Michigan and applied it to nearly every major business school in the world. As of this writing, Jeremy consults for and has licensed his premium LinkedIn content to over 150 of the world's top universities and other organizations, including Harvard Business School, Stanford Business School, London School of Business, INSEAD, Oxford, and more. While it was a long journey, this simple realization, a moment of openness, propelled Jeremy from a failed kindergarten teacher to a consultant to the world's top universities.

ABOUT THE BIG FIVE PERSONALITY TEST

You probably have a reasonable guess for where you fit on the openness scale, whether you tried one of the online Big Five personality tests* or not. However, this book is about transformation—so if you think you're low, high, or somewhere in the middle, know that the Big Five personality traits are not set in stone, and you can take steps to change them to enable any growth you seek. Furthermore, while the stories of those profiled here confirm the basic tenet that people who are open to new experiences are more likely to make amazing transformations (or be lucky), the way academic psychology measures openness has some inherent flaws you should be aware of. For example, a question on the Big Five personality test that serves as an input to openness is "Do you agree or disagree with the following statement (or something in between on a five-point scale)?": "I am full of ideas." One might think that because I've had a successful career in startup companies, been granted twenty-six patents, and have written a book, I must have answered "agree" to the statement. But I picked something in between. Sometimes I am full of ideas. Other times, I draw an absolute blank. It completely depends on the topic, who I'm with, how much sleep I had the night before, whether I had my coffee, and many other factors. The true answer to most of the questions on the Big Five personality test is "it depends." So, while these tests certainly measure something, they also miss a lot of nuance.

For scientific purposes, it's more convenient to simplify complex abstract concepts like personality traits into a numeric factor that can be correlated and analyzed. So, while, of course, the dynamics of everyone's personal level of openness is quite complicated, the openness personality trait is watered down to a single number between 0 and 100. The numeric simplicity has enabled countless academic studies centered on how the Big Five personality traits correlate to various behaviors. This is great, but depending on only

---

* Of the many "Big Five" tests I found, the one at https://openpsychometrics.org/ is free, uncommercialized, and works well.

the numbers to tell you what's going on is like looking at a box score the day after a basketball game. The box score can tell you a great deal about the game—who scored the most, had the most assists, and so on, but reading a box score is very different from watching the game. If you're at the game or even watch it on TV, you can see a much broader set of data that is really important but harder to quantify, like momentum swings, the effect of the crowd on the players and referees, and even tension between players. That's one of the reasons I combined in-depth stories of real people with the more quantitative academic studies in this book. You really need a little of both to understand the whole story.

OPENNESS IS A PRACTICE, NOT A TRAIT

The good news is that you're not locked into whatever you score on the openness personality scale. First, the "it depends" variables provide a nice window into how your mind works to best optimize for openness. So, if you are open to trying new foods or exploring different types of music, you have a sense of what it's like to be open on a topic. That feeling is something you can apply to other areas of your life. Second, if you are more open during different parts of the day or after activities like sleep, exercise, or eating, you have a level of control over it and can continue to improve it.

As we learned from Jeremy's experiences as a kindergarten teacher and at Teach for America, he was open to new ideas *only* after a painful failure. As Jeremy looked back on his career, he recounted, "The only really painful mistake is the one you keep repeating . . . like insanity." Now, with all these failures (a.k.a. experiences) under his belt, Jeremy tries to keep an open mind much earlier in any adverse situation than he did when he was younger. In fact, after our first interview, Jeremy confided to me that he's struggling in his current job, and our discussion reminded him to ask, "What can I open my eyes to?" So, openness is not only a personality trait but also a practice like yoga or meditation. Everyone has to continue to work on it, even the experts.

HOW TO CHANGE YOUR LEVEL OF OPENNESS

Given what we know from the quantitative world of psychology studies, there appear to be two ways that the openness personality trait can change. First, a forty-five-year longitudinal study[32] indicated that openness follows an inverted U-shape pattern over the average person's lifespan. On average, openness is lower earlier in life, peaks between the ages of forty to sixty, and then diminishes thereafter. So, if you're under sixty, chances are you're either on an openness upswing or near the top of your natural game.

But what if you want to go beyond your natural level of openness? According to a variety of studies, from college students[33] to older adults,[34] people who have the will to change their openness can. While the techniques studied in some of these academic papers are a bit constrained by the requirement to measure in statistically significant ways, perhaps the most grounded of the studies is by Mathias Allemand and Christoph Flückiger of the University of Zurich,[35] which concretely describes four steps people can take to change their level of openness:

1. **Raise awareness between your current and desired level of openness.** A great first step to raising your awareness might be taking an online Big Five personality test to understand your starting point and then rereading this chapter.

2. **Build on existing strengths.** Even if you're not consistently open, noticing areas where you are (like trying new recipes or traveling) can help you expand that openness to other domains.

3. **Reflect on beliefs or motives that could inhibit openness.** Think about why your level of openness is lower than you'd like. Was it part of your upbringing or influence from a parent or other important person in your life?

4. **Practice open behaviors.** By practicing these behaviors, you can change your outlook on life.

    a. Taking different routes to work every day.

    b. Saying "yes" to new opportunities or invitations you'd normally say no to.

    c. Trying new experiences outside your comfort zone such as a class on an unfamiliar topic.

    d. Seeking out new types of people you wouldn't normally interact with.

The stories and research in this chapter illustrate the power of openness as an aid to working through the Bumpy Part of the learning curve to get to the productive, steep part. As we saw from Isabel's, Helen's, and Jason's stories, it's also an important tool for finding your purpose. Being open to new experiences, ideas, and possibilities can unite you with opportunities you never knew existed. In addition, part of openness is a willingness to act on opportunities that come your way versus letting them slip through your fingers. Of course, there will be times when pursuing an opportunity has negative consequences too, but that's the price of making progress. While openness is often thought of as an inborn personality trait, it is also a practice you can cultivate. You can become more open by staying curious, trying new things, and being willing to change course. As the subjects profiled here show, embracing openness can empower you to follow wildly unexpected paths and lead to a more fulfilling and impactful life.

PRACTICAL GUIDE/SUMMARY

- Openness is one of the Big Five personality traits. People high on this scale are open to the kinds of transformations of those profiled in this book.

- Use A/B testing techniques or some less rigorous form of it to mitigate risk in life decisions or major transformations. Be open to surprising results.

- Be open to approaches that might sound crazy or have a low probability of working. This is where you might uncover unique methods or approaches others may have discounted.

- Volunteer to learn about and test your interest in a new area. Doing things for free is a great way to reduce the pressure of learning and mitigate the risk of transitioning to something new.

- People high on the openness scale are "lucky" because they give themselves more opportunities to "luck into" chance positive events.

- The openness personality trait is conducive to people saying "yes" to unique opportunities when presented versus letting them slip by.

- Use failure as an opportunity to open your mind to new ways of thinking or approaches.

- Openness is a practice you can improve, not just an inborn trait. Try new things and ask, "What can I open my eyes to?"

For more extensive guidance and exercises to increase your level of openness, check out the *Outsmart the Learning Curve Workbook* at https://www.outsmartbook.com/workbook or use the QR code below. It includes a short form openness quiz to gauge your current level of openness.

CHAPTER 3
GET HELP

Being likable greases the skids of life.
—Joe Sipher

WHEN I STARTED thinking about this book, before doing any real research or interviewing anyone, I assumed that "getting a coach" would be one of the most impactful tools to get through the Bumpy Part of a learning curve. I've benefited from formal and informal coaches all my life and have been a coach myself in many forms. But I hadn't been the recipient of formal coaching in a while. I was so certain that coaching would be important to the book that I hired a voice coach to experience the process of getting help outside my comfort zone (and in part because my wife and I created a parody music video toast for our daughter's wedding, and we *really* needed a voice coach). I also hired a writing coach to help me with this book because I am such a neophyte in the world of writing and publishing, and I planned to incorporate the story about how I used a coach to get through the learning curve of book writing—a kind of recursive subplot as evidence of the larger point.

While both of my recent coaching experiences have been excellent, after conducting dozens of interviews and working through a fair amount of tedious publication research, I was surprised to find that paying someone as a formal coach was not central to anyone's story in this book, and there appear to be much better (and often freer) ways to get help that were either the lynchpin to people's transformations or at a minimum made a significant difference. Sometimes, people found help from family and close friends; sometimes, that help came through networking, and sometimes, help just came to them in surprising ways. For example, Martha Niño realized her new purpose the moment she connected with that teary-eyed boy at a place like Adobe. Well before that day, Martha made her own amazing transformation: from silenced undocumented immigrant to successful corporate manager and inspiring advocate for those who came after her. She couldn't have done that without some help.

SEEKING A NEW LIFE

Like the boy she met at Adobe that day, Martha started her life on a farm, though hers was in a tiny rural village in the center of Mexico. Martha's parents were married as teenagers and barely able to get by working in the cotton fields. The young family lived in a grass shack with dirt floors until Martha's parents realized they had no future in Mexico. Martha's grandfather had immigrated to the small town of Niles, California, years before. Somehow, he had enough money left over from his job as a soap factory janitor to send cash back to each of his eight children in Mexico. Martha's grandfather told his daughter that jobs were plentiful in the US and that she and her husband could get paid $2 an hour (yes, that was the California minimum wage in 1975). Martha's parents calculated $2 per hour, at forty hours a week, times two people—they were going to be rich!

When President Lyndon Johnson signed the Hart-Celler Immigration Act in October of 1965, he said, "This bill we sign today is not a revolutionary bill. It does not affect the lives of millions. It will not restructure the shape of our daily lives." Johnson's prediction could not have been further from the truth.

The framework of Hart-Celler remains intact today and has affected millions of people for nearly six decades.[36] Countless modifications to this immigration law have, by and large, decreased quotas and made the parameters around legal immigration more stringent. At the same time, immigration enforcement has continued to become more sophisticated and harsher for those caught crossing the border without proper documentation.

Since the early 1900s, the most common way to get through this complicated and dangerous path to the US was to hire a "coyote" who knew the safest routes and timing of treacherous border crossings.[37] The coyote Martha's parents hired refused to let them bring eighteen-month-old Martha. He felt bringing her would increase the likelihood they would be caught and endanger the lives of the whole group. The most common way to smuggle young children across the border was for a female coyote with legal documentation to pose as the mother and drive the child across the border. Of course, Martha's parents were reticent to hand their only child over to a stranger—they had heard stories of parents never being reunited with their children on the other side. Yet, when they considered their harsh lives picking cotton in Mexico, they felt they had no choice. They agreed that a new life in the US was worth taking this daunting risk for. They handed baby Martha over to the stranger.

After what felt like days of fear and uncertainty, Martha was reunited with her parents in San Diego. The family eventually settled in a one-bedroom apartment in Niles with nine people living together. Given a powerful survival instinct, along with a fear of being sent back to Mexico, Martha's parents worked any job they could find: construction, babysitting, sewing clothes—simply anything they could get without a requirement to speak English fluently or the possibility of being reported as an undocumented immigrant. The work ethic was clear and ingrained into Martha's psyche from an early age, as was the directive to stay silent: "You were given the advice to be quiet, to lay low, to not say anything, ever. As a matter of fact, this story of my beginnings, of passing over the border . . . is rarely spoken because it's taboo and embarrassing for a lot of people." In over forty years, Martha never spoke a word of her harrowing border crossing and early years as an undocumented immigrant until she met that boy on Adobe's campus.

BE LIKABLE

By age ten, Martha was still living in that Niles apartment with eight other people. Martha went to elementary school with all the other kids in the neighborhood,* but she couldn't participate in extracurricular activities because her parents couldn't read the fliers that came home, and if there was any cost associated with the activity, her parents couldn't pay. But Martha had lots of energy, and one day, someone asked if any of the kids wanted to pick up a paper route after school. Martha enthusiastically volunteered, viewing it as an opportunity to get out of that cramped apartment, and she had been instilled with a deep work ethic from an early age. Delivering newspapers around the neighborhood gave young Martha her first taste of the business world, the experience she would build on for decades to come.

Martha started with one paper route and realized that if she could squeeze in a second route, she could double her income. Later, she started subcontracting her little brothers to do even more routes. But more importantly, she started understanding the value of people skills. Sometimes, customers would ask her to make sure the paper made it all the way to the porch, and when she obliged, occasionally, they'd give her a tip! Another part of her job was to make sure each customer renewed their subscription. Martha learned that being calm and patient with each customer helped ensure she'd get the subscription renewed.

Today, Martha almost always has an underlying smile on her

---

* The Equal Protection Clause of the 14th Amendment, supported by the 1982 Supreme Court decision in Plyler v. Doe, guarantees that all students, regardless of immigration status, have equal access to an education.

face that regularly erupts into a little laugh. While I've already documented some tough years when it must have been difficult to smile, in the past two decades of occasional interactions with her,* she has always been filled with smiles, bright eyes, curiosity, and empathy—even when she was laid off from her job in 2002.

This chapter is named "Get Help," which implies you have to explicitly seek help. But I've observed that for likable people, *help magically comes to them.* It probably isn't surprising that likability has been shown to increase a willingness to collaborate,[38] positively bias teacher evaluations,[39] and make expert witnesses more persuasive to juries in trial.[40] While I was unable to find a generalizable or meta-study to back this up, I'd argue that being likable can help with nearly any human interaction, particularly with those you don't know or don't know well. Martha was (and is) likable—she can't help it. In fact, every subject in this book is likable. As you'll see, likability was an underlying success factor in all their transformations, partly because their likability attracted help and opportunity from others.

Of course, this finding may be biased by the fact that if I didn't find a particular subject candidate likable, I probably would be less inclined to write about them. But that also proves my point—being likable greases the skids of life. It's well-documented that attractiveness[41] and height[42] also grease the skids of life, but those attributes are much harder to change, and generally, they go in the wrong direction as you get older. This book is about what you *can* change, and not only is likability essentially a skill you can come up the learning curve on, but it's also one that you get to keep for life and even improve as you get older. It took me a long time to figure this out, and frankly, I'm still working on it.

From middle school to graduate school, I didn't make many new friends. But when I did finally build a deeper relationship with someone, they would often later admit, "When we first met, I

---

* Martha and I worked together at Handspring between 2000 and 2002.

thought you were stuck up/conceited/aloof." The truth is I was the opposite of conceited; I feared being scrutinized or judged negatively by others and was filled with social self-doubt. As such, I didn't make much eye contact with people I didn't know well, rarely initiated small talk, and only greeted someone when they greeted me first. My excuse was that I'm an introvert, but anyone can learn likability skills, whether an introvert or extrovert. It may be harder for us introverts, but we can do it. Of course, the value of likability is that it leads to more human connections, leading to more opportunities to "luck" into serendipitous events.

For many of you, the following tips to increase likability may seem like natural human behavior. For others, these suggestions might feel scary and overwhelming. If following these tips feels a little uncomfortable, start small and work through the low-risk practice techniques.

- **Smile and make eye contact**—studies show smiling makes you more approachable,[43] and eye contact indicates interest, confidence, and trustworthiness.[44] It also makes you feel better about yourself.[45] To practice, simply walk down a busy street and attempt to make eye contact with people coming the other way. If you can catch their eye, smile. If you're an introvert like me, you'll be shocked at how many people smile back. I stumbled on this exercise because I often walk around my hometown of San Francisco listening to podcasts. One day, someone smiled at me for no apparent reason, but then I realized I must have been smiling because I had just heard something funny on the podcast. For practice, I go out of my way to make eye contact and smile in every city I visit. Different cultures yield different results, but so far, I can get some people to smile just about everywhere. And, of course, use your instincts! If you come across someone you wouldn't want to have a subsequent interaction with, don't make eye contact or smile.

- **Use positive body language**—besides smiling and making eye contact, a meta-study out of Harvard and Boston University[46] found that several simple but powerful cues can increase likability and rapport with another person, including the following:

  - **Posture mirroring**—adopting similar positions to the person you're chatting with or making similar postural changes around the same time.

  - **Forward trunk lean**—this means leaning toward the person you're conversing with.

  - **Direct body orientation**—facing the person squarely versus at an angle.

  - **Uncrossed arms**—crossed arms indicate being closed off.

  - **Head nodding—when appropriate.** Constant head nodders may cause the opposite effect.

  I've found that adopting these nonverbal practices starts out a bit awkward because you're conscious of it at first, but over time, it becomes natural.

- **Ask questions and actively listen**—asking questions and actively listening makes people feel valued and understood. One of my favorite recent books is *Never Split the Difference*[47] by Chris Voss, a former FBI hostage negotiator. It's intended to be a book about negotiation, but it helped me with a much broader range of human interaction. You'd think an FBI hostage negotiator would recommend a variety of strong-arm techniques. But Voss found that the hard-ass negotiation style simply doesn't work. Instead, the book is filled with softer approaches, including asking a lot of open-ended questions that begin with "what" and "how" to build rapport with your negotiation partner. To practice, initiate a conversation with an acquaintance you don't know well or even a stranger by asking a question that can't be answered with a yes or no, like, "How do you like the neighborhood?" or "Do you have a favorite spot to grab coffee around here?" The idea is to find common ground in the setting/activity and keep it casual. Maybe more important than the question is the active listening part. Don't have your next question chambered up before they finish their answer. Make sure your next question is related and communicates an understanding of what they just said. Again, this may be obvious to some but difficult for others to execute at first.

- **Be helpful**—reciprocity, the practice of exchanging things with others for mutual benefit, appears to be an innate feature of our species going back to prehistoric times.[48] Countless studies have confirmed the reciprocity principle in various circumstances and across cultures. So, if you're helpful, someone will be more likely to help you. If you see someone carrying too much or dropping something, offer to help them. If you see someone who seems lost, offer to point them in the right direction. If it makes sense, ask them an open-ended question to start a conversation. Helping strangers will feel good in and of itself. However, with enough occurrences, reciprocity is likely to come into play eventually, and maybe one of these people will become an important contact in business or in life.

These are just a few suggestions for increasing likability. For a deeper exploration beyond eye contact and a smile, I recommend *The 11 Laws of Likability*[49] by Michelle Tillis Lederman.

SOMEONE WHO BELIEVES IN YOU

Most of the subjects profiled here said they wouldn't have made it without the help of an important person who gave them an opportunity or showed them the way to success. Each person had a different word for it ("mentor," "angel," and "believer"), but they all described a pivotal individual who guided, inspired, and supported them through the Bumpy Parts of their most difficult learning curve. For some, the believer was a partner or spouse; for others, it was a relative stranger who seemed to pluck the person from a crowd and shower them with opportunity. In some cases, the lucky recipient of a believer's opportunity had no idea why they were chosen (e.g., why was Jeremy the one Teach for America fellow out of forty selected for the special project to recruit outside of top universities?). In retrospect, I suspect a simple combination of being likable, showing enthusiasm, and taking action when the opportunity arose made these subjects attractive to the believer.

• • •

By fourteen, Martha was getting a little too old for the paper route. "When guys start whistling out in the street, that's when you know it's time to change careers." Martha's mother had started working in the warehouse of a ceramics company. She wanted to keep Martha close, so she found her a job in the warehouse after school. Martha's energy worked against her in the ceramics factory, though—too often, she accidentally bumped into things or dropped work-in-process lamps or figurines. One day, as she was sweeping up one of her ceramic messes, the company's owner, Beth Hines, approached her.

Martha feared she would be fired, but Beth saw something beyond the accident-prone teenager—she clearly saw something else she liked about Martha. As Martha described it, Beth, with her "blond hair, blue eyes, and pearls," asked Martha, with her "80's style high hair and blue eyeshadow," to come to the front office and answer phones. "That right there was the biggest life-changing moment . . . ever." Fourteen-year-old Martha had no idea what to do in a front office, but Beth patiently guided her through the basic office functions, like answering phones and filing, and Martha was hooked.

"I was kind of addicted to being there because it was warm [the warehouse was always freezing], there were free donuts, and there was free everything—things I didn't have at my house. Although my mom was working in the back of the warehouse, I felt like she was proud of me for being in the front office."

Beth needed some typing done, but Martha didn't know how to type, so she asked Martha if there was a typing class at her school. There was, and Martha signed up. It's notable that such a mundane suggestion (and the follow-through from Martha) solidified Martha's place in the office world versus a manual labor world that may have been her destiny. The skill of typing put Martha ahead of many of her peers at the time. As Martha proved herself to be a reliable worker, willing to learn new skills, Beth continued to give Martha more responsibilities. First, it was handling the paperwork for accounts payable, then dealing with accounts receivable. Not too long after that, Martha started calling delinquent customers and using her charm to get them to pay the bills. Beth walked her through every one of these new skills while Martha was still fourteen or fifteen years old.

"She was super patient with me and spoke to me as if I was an adult, not a child. That really resonated with me because I felt like I was doing something that maybe other people couldn't, and she believed I could."

Beth was a believer in every sense of the word. Martha didn't mention many Bumpy Parts of the learning curve during this stage in her life in part because Beth mentored her through any difficulties. Beth was doing right by her company by employing a minimum-wage teenager to handle a bunch of clerical work, and at the same time, she was giving young Martha the skills and confidence that would propel the rest of her career. When I asked Martha why she thought Beth picked her to move to the office, after thinking about it, she, completely unprompted, practically recited the "Be Likable" section above: she was always a friendly person who smiled, made eye contact, and listened to what others had to say. Some of these behaviors came naturally, and some came from the skills she learned working with her customers on the paper route. She conjectured that Beth picked her because she felt she would be easy to work with and easy to train as compared to the other kids working in the warehouse at the time.

CULTIVATE A SUPPORT SYSTEM

While working at the ceramics factory built Martha's confidence and reinforced the importance of a great work ethic, school was a different story for her. Education was not central to her family's values. For Martha, high school was a nuisance that took time away from her very complicated, serious life. Martha's father was dying of cancer, so Martha picked up more work responsibilities while her mother helped nurse her father. During this same time, her fourteen-year-old brother's girlfriend got pregnant, and the family had to deal with the complications. These more important life issues led to Martha not focusing on school, not doing her homework, and often not showing up. By her senior year, she was kicked out of her high school for academic reasons.

No teacher or school counselor asked, "What's going on?" or tried to guide her through this rough patch. She was just redirected to the district's "continuation school." California created the continuation school system for students at risk of not graduating at the normal pace. The graduation requirements are the same, but students are allowed to earn their credits over a longer period. Every one of the students at Martha's continuation school was going through something: some were homeless, others were children of parents with drug problems, and others had drug problems themselves. As Martha said, "None of these kids were bad. They were just going through stuff."

On her first day at the continuation school, a counselor met with Martha and asked her why she was redirected to this school. In typical teenage fashion, Martha said she "was kicked out of school for whatever." She put up a tough-girl wall because her experience with school administrators was that they really didn't care. Frankly, she was indifferent about graduating anyway. Unlike the principal at her previous school, the counselor didn't give in to her teenage combativeness. He knew everyone had a story, and he wanted to get to the bottom of Martha's. He asked her about her home life, if she worked, what caused her to miss so much school. After a few more rounds of being reticent, Martha finally let loose: her father was dying, she had to pick up the workload to help the family, and her little brother got a girl pregnant. She just didn't have enough time for school.

Once the counselor understood Martha's situation and constraints, he outlined a plan that would enable Martha to graduate with her classmates at her old school even though she was nearly a year behind. Getting back to her school and graduating on time motivated Martha—she wanted to prove to the principal and her classmates that she could do it, plus she would also be the first high school graduate in her family. So Martha agreed to the counselor's plan, which focused on the classes she needed for graduation. The counselor guided her through the complications of limited availability classes by sending her to night school for some of the classwork.

The one sticky point about the counselor's plan was that some classes interfered with her schedule at the ceramics factory. Martha needed to continue to make money for the family, but she still wanted to graduate. With trepidation, Martha told Beth the whole story. Beth was completely supportive. She wanted Martha to graduate and gave her the opportunity to work on weekends to make up for lost time while catching up to her high school peers. Not only did Martha have a believer in Beth, but she had also built (or allowed into her life through likability and vulnerability) a powerful little support system that enabled her to graduate on time and carry on with her career.

HOW AND WHEN TO GET HELP

About a year after Martha graduated from high school, Beth decided to move her operations to Arizona using a maquiladora structure. A maquiladora is a corporate facility that literally straddles the US-Mexican border such that the parent company is located on the US side and the manufacturing operation is on the Mexican side. This approach allows for cheaper manufacturing in Mexico while reducing duty costs when moving the goods to the US. Beth offered Martha the job of helping to manage the maquiladora in Arizona—a huge opportunity—but Martha could not leave her family after her father passed away and her new nephew was born. So she said goodbye to Beth, never to see her again.

After leaving Beth's company, Martha bounced around a bit before landing at Adobe. In a relatively short time, Martha went from figuring out how many screws it took to build a cubicle to representing her company at an electronics trade show and managing the process of creating smartphone "dummy units" displayed in retail stores like Walmart. Every step of the way, there were two themes to Martha's approach to finding and becoming effective at each job: 1) when she was faced with an unfamiliar situation or had to learn a new skill, her first thought was always, *I'll figure it out.* Through her experience on the paper route and with Beth, Martha had built a level of self-confidence that she could figure out just about anything, and 2) she cultivated and relied on her support system and network *well* to both find her new roles and—as importantly—to find people to help her learn the necessary skills to get good at her job.

• • •

There are countless books and articles about using your network—it's kind of an obvious truism to rely on your network to find jobs and get help. Yet I've mentored many college graduates and young professionals over the years, and when I recommend creative ways of leveraging their network, they often nod and smile and say they will, but many of them absolutely don't. Later, when probing as to why they haven't taken advantage of their network (or mine via LinkedIn), it boils down to 1) they really don't have a clear plan on how to network, and 2) many have a hard time putting themselves in the vulnerable position of asking for help. Let's address the "how" part first.

A study led by University of Minnesota researcher Connie R. Wanberg attempted to answer the question "Can job seekers achieve more through networking?"[50] The answer is "yes" (duh), but the researcher's methodology may prove to be more helpful than the study's somewhat surprising results. The researchers separated 491 unemployed people into two randomly assigned groups. While the control group received no extra help, the "intervention" group was given quite a useful and structured networking plan that required each person to

- Create an "elevator pitch" to concisely explain their background and job search goals. Participants were able to practice their elevator pitches and get feedback.

- Contact 100 percent of their close personal connections and inform them of their job search using the practiced elevator pitch. This effort mobilized their networks and allowed them to seek advice from their contacts.

- Extend their networks beyond close ties to secondary connections using tools like LinkedIn.

- Develop a two-week plan to go beyond their close contacts, including specific contacts, reasons for contacting them, and conversation starters.

- Reflect on potential networking barriers like lack of confidence and develop strategies to overcome them.

This networking plan seems excellent and is one that I would recommend. However, the surprising finding in this study was that the intervention group did not find jobs at a statistically significantly higher rate than the control group. The researchers blamed a hot job market at the time of the study in 2017, so everyone was getting jobs. However, the intervention group rated the quality of their new jobs statistically significantly higher than their previous jobs and reported statistically significantly higher salaries. Either way, the researcher's structured networking method is an excellent guide for anyone looking to utilize their network, whether to find a job, seek help, or increase your chances of finding an opportunity you didn't even know you were interested in.

The *Luck Factor* guy, Richard Wiseman, noted that lucky people maintain stronger networks than unlucky ones. This is why maintaining your network is something I recommend as a regular practice rather than only when you need it. Setting aside time for regular reach-outs to former colleagues, friends, and family members not only helps you maintain relationships, which, of course, has its own intrinsic value, but it keeps that stream of opportunities flowing that you'd never know about unless you kept in touch.

This is all great, but you must execute the excellent plan above or something like it to build and cultivate your network. The last bullet of the plan above—"reflect on potential networking barriers like lack of confidence..."—is an indicator that the researchers found what I did—that with all the tips, encouragement, and opportunity in the world, people still often don't network as much as they could. Between experience with my mentees, my adult children, and my own insecurities, there appear to be three distinct but related problems people run into:

1. Asking for help requires being vulnerable and is one way of saying, "I can't do this by myself." Admitting weakness like this is hard, especially for men.[51]

2. Reaching out to your network almost always includes some level of rejection. Not everyone will respond, and that doesn't feel great.

3. I often hear, "I don't want to bug people or be a nuisance," which can be interpreted as people don't want to invest their time in helping me.

If you're a natural networker and none of the issues above bother you, feel free to skip to the next section.

GETTING OVER THOSE BUMPY NETWORKING HURDLES

The good news is that we can address each of these Bumps on the networking learning curve with some simple yet powerful tips. If reaching out and asking for help makes you feel vulnerable, don't ask for help (at least not to start). Remember that networking is mutually beneficial. By making or rekindling a connection, you could be bringing something to your contacts that they would have never known unless you reached out. Before making any ask, remember the reciprocity principle: focus on what's going on in their life and how you can help them. Last, when you do ask, remember that your vulnerability can actually strengthen your connection—being open about needing help can make you more relatable.

Regarding rejection, I've found two strategies that can help. First, start with closer friends and family—they should be more likely to respond than people you have more distant connections with or no connections at all. Starting with closer connections will help with confidence and allow you to practice and improve your pitch for the more difficult task of reaching out to distant contacts or strangers.

The second strategy to better deal with rejection is to simply reframe people not responding to the "conversion rate." When salespeople or marketers reach out to find new customers, they actually assume a huge rejection rate. As sales and marketing people, they reposition rejection as more palatable—a conversion rate. That is, a 90 percent rejection rate is equal to a 10 percent conversion rate. A 10 percent conversion rate would be considered outstanding for most sales or marketing campaigns. Apply this same logic to your networking; just assume that some large percentage of people won't respond and recognize that's normal.

On the third issue of assuming people don't want to be bothered, Stanford researcher Xuan Zhao and her colleague Nicholas Epley from the University of Chicago conducted a compelling 2022 study that showed just the opposite: *Surprisingly Happy to Have Helped: Underestimating Prosociality Creates a Misplaced Barrier to Asking for Help.*[52]

The researchers ran six different experiments across over 2,000 subjects, the most interesting of which was held at a public botanical garden in which a volunteer subject (the *asker*) was required to ask a stranger (the *helper*) to take their photo in front of a pond at a public botanical garden. Before requesting the photo, the *asker* first had to estimate, among other things,

1. How willing the *helper* would be to take their photo.

2. What motivated *helpers* to help? Being altruistic, based on social pressure, or the awkwardness of saying "no."

3. How inconvenienced *helpers* might feel about the request.

After the photo was taken (96 percent of the *helpers* said yes), *askers* asked the *helper* to fill out a survey rating their actual feelings about the interaction. The *askers'* forecast of the *helpers'* perception of the interaction was terrible. They essentially assumed the worst in people.

Specifically, *askers*:

1. Underestimated the *helpers'* willingness to help by 16 percent.

2. Underestimated *helpers'* altruistic motivation to help by 57 percent.

3. Overestimated how inconvenienced the *helpers* felt by more than six times!

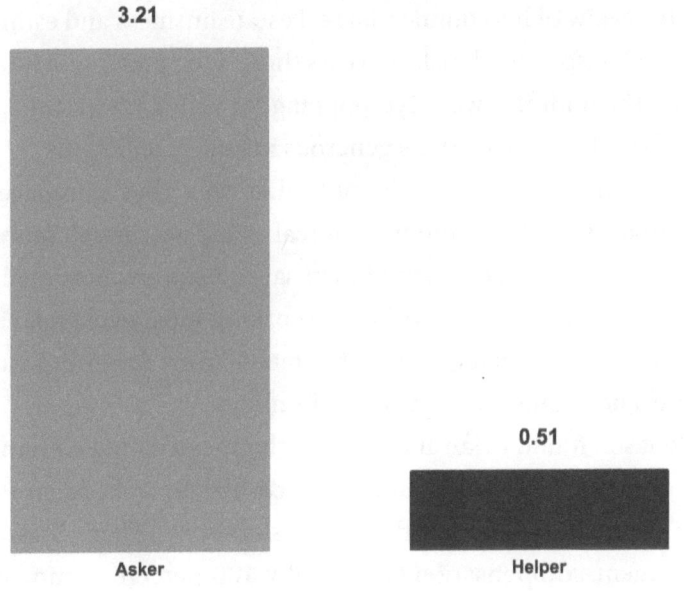

Figure 4—Perceived Inconvenience (0–10 scale)

Like most academic studies, we cannot extrapolate this one to every situation. That said, people generally want to help for the right reasons and don't feel inconvenienced at all. So go ahead and ask!

JASON FINDS HIS MENTOR

After Jason Lee had his magic-mushroom-inspired vision to become a real estate mogul as a college junior, he didn't instantly become one. Jason had zero knowledge of the real estate industry and zero network to help him build that knowledge. His first action was joining the San Diego State Real Estate Club. The first club-sponsored event Jason attended was a "speed dating" setup with twenty college students and twenty real estate professionals. Each pairing had two minutes to get to know each other before meeting someone new. Jason's first seven "dates" didn't go that great. On the eighth, he met Brian Nelson, "the only guy there who was there to truly hire someone." Brian shared a clear overview of his commercial real estate business and estimated how much Jason could make in years three, four, and five, if he stuck with it. The numbers were eye-popping for young Jason (though he would later blow past Brian's generous income predictions).

The other nuance Brian provided was that compared to residential real estate, commercial real estate* was much more of a logical return on investment kind of sale versus an emotional one. There would be no open houses or working long weekends. Jason thought that if he could learn this much from Brian in just two minutes, he should follow up with him.

So Jason found Brian at the end of the speed dating session, and after one more interview, Brian invited him to start as an intern while Jason finished his last three semesters at San Diego State. Real estate agent compensation is generally 100 percent commission-based. That is, if you don't make a sale, you don't make any money. And Jason couldn't make a sale in those first few months because he hadn't even passed the California real estate exam. While studying for the real estate exam and learning everything he could from Brian, Jason needed cash. He stumbled on a YouTube "side hustle" video that described how to connect with local restaurants and help them

---

* If you've heard commercial real estate is in trouble given the post-pandemic acceleration of remote work, it's the office space segment of commercial real estate that's really struggling. Brian and Jason both focus on the multifamily home segment—essentially buying and selling multiunit apartment complexes. This area of commercial real estate has been doing relatively well, particularly in San Diego County, all through the pandemic.

advertise on Facebook. Based on this video, Jason essentially started a digital advertising business. He searched for local restaurants that had no social or web presence, then cold-called them. Once he got ahold of the right person, he pitched them on how he could increase their customer base by building a digital footprint and drawing customers via online advertising.

To make this business work, Jason had to learn all about building websites and the basics of Facebook advertising to drum up business for these local restaurants. While this side hustle allowed him to make a little cash during his financial drought, Jason didn't really love the business or working with his advertising clients. As soon as he started making money through real estate, he dropped out of this business. However, the experience proved invaluable in real estate later.

TAKING A NEW APPROACH

Jason spent three years at Brian's real estate firm. For the first year and a half, he was still going to school while putting in twenty to thirty hours a week in the office. He spent much of that time "on the flywheel," making lots and lots of cold calls, which yielded some number of appointments, and of those appointments, a small percentage led to a relationship with either an investor or a seller. An even smaller number of those relationships resulted in a transaction. Jason called this "the archaic way" of doing real estate, which is the way Brian taught him and how commercial real estate agents have acquired customers for decades.

While Jason and his team continue to employ this archaic methodology to this day, he understood something the forty-, fifty-, and sixty-year-olds at old-school commercial real estate firms like CBRE and Marcus and Millichap didn't. Jason could scale his outreach in an incredibly powerful way using technology. In his advertising side hustle, he learned that a little bit of digital advertising can drive customers to social media accounts and that social media can exponentially increase awareness of demographics you're interested in.

Early on, Jason started an informative real estate-focused podcast as well as an entertaining and insightful YouTube channel, which has garnered a healthy subscriber base. The podcasts and videos don't close any business for him, but they build awareness and—more importantly—credibility. Jason understood that when you're twenty-something in a business filled with competitors more than twice your age, you need credibility. "I've won a decent number of listings just because they listen to one podcast or one of my YouTube videos. It's one way I've actually stood apart from my competitors."

Jason started his YouTube channel while working at Brian's firm as he continued to have success using the archaic approach of cold-calling for business. After three years, Jason had many transactions under his belt and relationships with deep-pocketed investors who believed in Jason. One of those investors felt so strongly about Jason's abilities that he agreed to partner with him on a new real estate firm. The partners would both invest 50 percent into the business to start. The duo had complementary skill sets—Jason would be the face of the company and acquire new investors and sellers. His silent partner provided a "big balance sheet" and handled all critical backend operations like debt financial analysis and taxes.

WHO, NOT HOW

Even with a more experienced partner, Jason's move to start his own commercial real estate agency was quite bold, given his level of experience. He was a twenty-three-year-old competing with people who had twenty, thirty, or more years of experience. While he knew he had a powerful tool in using digital techniques to build his reputation and customer base, he also knew there was a ton he didn't know. Jason was able to rely on his new business partner for backend support, but he didn't have his mentor, Brian, to depend on for the outbound and transactional activities he was responsible for. So he had to find help another way.

Jason's approach to solving problems is "If you want to learn how to do something, don't ask yourself how. Ask yourself *who* can help me do this thing." When faced with a new issue, instead of racking his brain to figure out how to solve the problem, Jason thinks about who might have solved this problem before. First, he thinks about people in his network, and if no one in his close circle can help, he reaches out to make new connections with experts. By finding the right person to help him, Jason often solves the problem quicker than if he had tried to do it himself. While sometimes this is free advice, and sometimes he has to pay an expert, Jason certainly gets through the Bumpy Part of the learning curve more efficiently than if he tried it alone.

Martha used a similar technique of seeking peer coaches when she had to learn new skills for each new job she found herself thrown into, from the ceramics factory to the cubicle company to the digital hardware media company to the smartphone company. "The way you figure out things is you ask questions of your peers or experts in different parts of the company." Martha often asked peers rather than her manager because they often knew more details about the topic than management, and she didn't have to worry about any repercussions about asking her manager "dumb questions"—not that there should be for any good manager, but not all managers are as tolerant and helpful as Beth was.

MASTERING MASTERMINDS

Jason went further than just asking around and moving on to get help. He found that cultivating relationships with peers provided significantly more value. It started with him following top commercial real estate agents in the multifamily segment on various social media sites. When he found a person who was really inspiring, compelling, or implementing new approaches he hadn't seen before, Jason would reach out and make a personal connection. Since most of the people he followed lived and worked outside of San Diego, they were interested in hearing about the booming San Diego market, and Jason was interested in their unique approaches in their locales. They'd get together in real time or via Zoom to compare notes and share advice for all aspects of the business. "Hearing how they think, how they do things, really moved the needle for me." Jason formed this group organically, but there's a name for what he created: a "mastermind group."

The 1928 book *The Law of Success in Sixteen Lessons*[53] by Napoleon Hill is the first to mention the concept of a mastermind group. Hill was a kind of Tony Robbins of his day: receiving vast sums for motivational speeches around the country, palling around with the likes of Andrew Carnegie and Henry Ford, and eventually becoming an adviser to Franklin D. Roosevelt. Hill defined a mastermind group as "the harmonious cooperation of two or more people who ally themselves for the purpose of accomplishing any given task." The definition has evolved over time to a peer-to-peer mentoring group with four to eight members who meet regularly to share ideas, give feedback, and help each other solve problems. The members of the group often have the same job function (e.g., salespeople, teachers, or entrepreneurs), so each is already familiar with the broader issues and problem-solving approaches of that function, but the members are not competitive with each other. The sessions can be in person or virtual, but one member of the group is usually assigned the role of moderator to keep discussions flowing between topics and members.

I was first introduced to the idea of a mastermind group through an organization called On Deck, which bills itself as a global community of top product, engineering, and entrepreneurial talent who are about to start their next thing. I joined the Founders program, which starts as an intensive eight-week session for people about to start a new company. While On Deck also includes an incredibly active community message board, a directory of members from all cohorts, and a library of hundreds of previous presentations, perhaps the most valuable part for me (and many others) was an eight-person mastermind group where each member could both air out issues about their business and help others along their journeys. The experience was both gratifying and valuable—in many ways more helpful than one-on-one consults from mentors or other confidants. How do mastermind groups provide more value?

- **Less baggage around hard questions.** Since members of your mastermind group don't work with you or have a personal relationship with you, you can ask questions that might be uncomfortable for a manager, mentor, or partner. For example, "How do I deal with my overbearing boss?" or "How do I manage my struggle with work-life balance?" Of course, you can ask those questions of those closer to you, but you're more likely to get responses that are biased by their own agenda (e.g., your boss probably doesn't want you to quit, and your partner may have their own opinions about how much time you should spend at home).

- **Variety of perspectives.** The mastermind group exposes you to people with a wider range of viewpoints, experiences, and ideas than a single coach or mentor. The variety can help you see blind spots, challenge assumptions, and find solutions you might not have come up with on your own. The group can expose you to completely different ways of thinking compared to the echo chamber of your workplace or friend group. The group's combined knowledge, connections, and capabilities is almost like having a personal board of advisers.

- **A safe place to explore new ideas.** Ideas that aren't fully developed can sometimes get quashed early by existing teams or peers at work because the idea may not be aligned with someone's agenda, or perhaps the ideas need to be "workshopped" a bit. The mastermind group can help you develop ideas as a group, with no specific agenda about your task or job function.

- **Accountability.** When the group comes up with a consensus and action items on your issue, there is a higher level of accountability when you go back to the next session and report on what happened. My experience is that even a little external accountability leads to thinking through the ideas more thoroughly and executing them if they really make sense.

- **Builds your network.** Often, the mastermind group is made up of relative strangers. As you meet regularly and delve deeply into each other's issues, you build individual relationships. Mastermind members are often eager to offer help on an individual basis too. Mastermind groups promote a pay-it-forward mentality rather than just a one-way mentee-mentor dynamic.

Not all mastermind groups work as well as Jason's. In fact, I found quite polarizing opinions on the value of mastermind groups. While many people who experienced them found their groups incredibly valuable, others felt like their mastermind group was an awkward waste of time. With more research, what separated those two extremes were some simple guidelines when joining or creating a group. First and foremost, everyone has to commit to showing up to every meeting. If it's once a week, once a month, or once a quarter, everyone needs to agree on a time to show up. According to one mastermind expert, as soon as people stop attending, sometimes even a single session, trust starts to break down within the group, and trusting other members is key to maximizing the benefits of a mastermind. Without trust in each of the other members, people won't feel comfortable sharing their most vulnerable problems or may perhaps hold back details that might help everyone understand the whole picture. The benefits come when you can be completely open. Another mastermind organizer found that alignment on timing is even more important than aligning stages of career or personality types or *any* other criteria. The mastermind group will fail if people can't commit to a common time.

The second key to a successful mastermind is a common goal or theme. Jason's was obviously commercial real estate in the multifamily home segment. Within that context, people could talk about customer acquisition techniques, closing techniques, investing strategies, hiring, etc. Themes can be broader than that—for example, a functional role like product management, which could serve a wide range of products and services, or broader still, for example, people in the same stage of their career development. However, a common context sets a baseline of understanding for everyone.

This all sounds great, but how do you get into a mastermind group? One option is to join an existing organization, like I did with On Deck, that uses mastermind groups as a supporting tool. However, these organizations can be expensive, and many insist on a professional facilitator, which can help with the process early on but can also hurt the group by depending on the facilitator to drive everything forward and allowing members to take a back seat. Another option is to create one on your own, as Jason did. While clearly valuable in the end, his painstaking, cultivated approach, starting with zero for each member, building a relationship, and then adding to the group, took a long time. Another similar approach is to start with your own network. When you look at your LinkedIn connections or Facebook friends in this new light, you might find four or five people who are really at the same stage of development and trying to do the same things. Reach out with the mastermind values list above and see if you can bring them together. If you can't build a mastermind group from your network, there are other options, such as logging on to meetup.com and searching on the "group" tab for "mastermind" or even Googling "X mastermind group near me" where X is your goal or theme.

Once you've pulled your group together, a few basic guidelines will keep your group running smoothly and effectively for all the members. First, set a few general boundaries:

- **Keep it small.** The group should consist of between four and eight people. Fewer than four people will not provide the variety of opinions needed to make it work, and more than eight will become unwieldy.

- **Attendance required.** As noted above, get commitment from each member to meet consistently. More than once a week is probably overkill, and less often than quarterly may lead to people forgetting issues or drifting. Every other week seems to be a sweet spot.

- **Agree on ground rules.** Ground rules include topic inclusions and exclusions. For example, can topics cover both business and personal issues? Will people be comfortable sharing financial issues? Also, what is the confidentiality policy? It's generally recommended that everything inside the group be kept confidential.

- **Be supportive.** Everyone in the group needs to recognize it's their responsibility to support everyone else. Negative vibes will wreck the group.

- **Contribute.** Be open about your struggles. This will require some uncomfortable vulnerability, but you'll only grow and get feedback on the items you share. Also, share ideas, tools, and approaches that work for you. A mastermind group isn't the place to hold back information because "knowledge is power." Masterminds are about sharing knowledge to make other members better.

- **Be honest.** Part of being supportive is giving people bad news or providing honest advice that may be critical. You can be supportive and provide constructive criticism at the same time. Just be nice about it.

- **Keep it time-bound.** An hour is a good boundary here. Larger groups may need a little more time.

Running a mastermind session is pretty simple, whether in person or on a video call. Pick a moderator for each session—the responsibility should rotate among members to provide everyone an opportunity to practice leadership. The moderator may set a theme or topic before the meeting, but each session should start with each member giving a quick update on action items from the last session or new items they want to bounce off the group. Then, the moderator can decide to delve deeply into one of the member issues or move on to the predetermined topic. At the end of the session, each member commits to their follow-up item for the next meeting—accountability. A professional facilitator could help smooth out the meeting process, but if members can't handle these relatively simple moderator responsibilities, that may be a sign they won't be great contributors. It's important to note that mastermind groups don't last forever. They naturally fizzle out as objectives and careers change. Great value can be had in just a few months. I've also heard of mastermind groups lasting a decade or more.

BE OPEN TO WEAK TIES

When Jeremy and I first started talking about his career-changing event of learning how to use Excel as a recruiting tool for Teach for America candidates, he mentioned this pivotal person who opened his eyes to the power of using technology for marketing. Yet when I asked Jeremy that person's name, initially, Jeremy couldn't even remember that it was Christian. This incredibly pivotal person in Jeremy's life was not his manager, coach, or mentor but rather a fleeting relationship with a random guy who sat next to him for six months until Jeremy was put in a position where he needed to be open to help. Similarly, perhaps the most pivotal person in Isabel's life was the marketing executive and female pilot Eleanor Chen. However, Eleanor never gave Isabel any advice or mentored her through her journey to become a pilot and an aerospace engineer. And the moment with Microsoft Word product manager Melinda

(French) Gates that sparked my own career pivot was a similar loose connection that I never followed up on. I'm certain Melinda Gates has no idea who I am.

Back in the 1970s, Stanford sociologist Mark Granovetter theorized that weak ties are *more* valuable than close ones when it comes to career building.[54] The paper suggests that because closer connections have largely the same network as you do, they're less likely to help you find new connections. You and your close connections essentially know the same people, and finding new jobs or opportunities is about making new connections. The weaker connections provide bridges to other social networks, which in turn create more connection opportunities.

While it was one of the most cited papers in the social sciences over the last fifty years, the theory wasn't rigorously tested until 2022 when a group of LinkedIn data scientists and academic researchers analyzed the networks of over twenty million LinkedIn users over five years.[55] Their findings supported Granovetter's theory that weak ties are indeed more valuable than strong ones for job searches. In addition, the huge amount of data and their methodology enabled them to establish a causal relationship between the number of connections and job transactions and quantify what "weak tie" really means. The weakest ties, meaning people you have zero or one connection with, are actually not good at generating job opportunities, and of course, strong ties don't work well either because you have too many connections in common. The study found the sweet spot for the number of mutual LinkedIn friends to optimize job opportunities: ten. The data followed an inverted U-shaped curve with ten connections at the top and greater numbers of connections quickly tailing off.

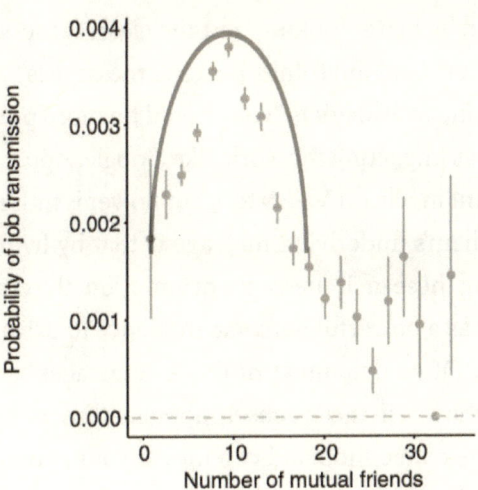

Figure 5—Optimal Number of Mutual Friends for Job Referrals

The point is that your network is not just your friends, family, or the people you work with. You can get help from a much broader group, but it's wise to look for those sweet-spot people with whom you have ten or so mutual connections. These people will lead you to opportunities that your close network cannot. In addition, look out for the inspirational person who may not lead you to a new job but can open your eyes to a new opportunity, a new way to solve a problem, or a path to transformation.

• • •

Computer scientist, investor, and essayist Paul Graham suggests that where you live can outsize your career and outlook. His 2008 essay "Cities and Ambition"[56] proposes that great cities attract ambitious people, and the cities send messages to their citizens in a magical, reciprocal way. The message the city sends depends on the root values of the city. For example, Graham says that New York tells its citizens "in a hundred subtle ways" that "you should make more money." His caveat is that "there are other messages too, of course. You should be hipper. You should be better looking. But the clearest message is that you should be richer." Graham thinks Boston's message is "you should be smarter," and Silicon Valley's is "you should be more powerful." I'll interpret "power" as impacting the world like Google, Apple, and Uber. Money is important in Silicon Valley too, but power is more central to its ambition. Graham's underlying message is that by living in these cities and receiving these tacit messages of ambition, the city in which you live can serve as a powerful personal influence to drive your own ambitions higher. Of course, most of those "messages" are coming from the people who live in these densely populated areas—the people you overhear at the coffee shop and run into at your gym. Living in a city with people who share your ambitions provides encouragement that helps you do great work. To me, an even higher value than the ambition to live in one of these metro areas is exposing yourself to talented, interesting people who are great candidates to create and build on loose connections.

Entrepreneur turned lifestyle guru Tim Ferriss agreed with Graham on a recent podcast but suggested that you don't have to move to New York, Boston, or Silicon Valley to access these networks.[57] However, he does recommend moving to a high-density population center. Good candidate metros may be midsized cities that have an important company headquarters, like Ottawa, home to Shopify, or Pittsburgh, where Duolingo is based. Of course, it's not easy to get up and move; however, if you're early in your career or it's time for a pivot, Ferriss suggests that the value of moving to a higher density area is likely worth the pain: "If you're serious, I think many people should consider moving to an area of high density for a period of time. It could be three months, it could be six months, could be longer."

Yes, a big decision—but something to seriously consider if you're in a transitional phase of your life.

PRACTICAL GUIDE/SUMMARY

- Seek out people who believe in you and provide opportunities. Be open to mentors coming from unexpected places.

- Likable people attract more help. Build relationships through kindness, empathy, and helpfulness. Ask "what" and "how" questions to activate real conversations.

- Help others when you can. Reciprocity means they'll be more likely to help you back. Pay it forward.

- Use your network for support and advice. Have a plan for networking, from your pitch to who to contact. Reframe rejections as conversion rates to measure your progress.

- Find experts who can shortcut your learning process. Learn from their experiences instead of figuring it out yourself.

- Join or create a mastermind group to get feedback and build accountability. Surround yourself with ambitious people trying to achieve similar goals.

- Be open to help from loose connections and "weak ties" (those connections with ten or so mutual friends). Serendipitous meetings can change your life. Put yourself in positions to make it easy for them to help.

- Consider moving to a metro area with people who share your ambitions. Cities send messages that can support your goals.

For more extensive guidance and exercises on getting help, check out the *Outsmart the Learning Curve Workbook* at https://www.outsmartbook.com/workbook or use the QR code below.

CHAPTER 4
CONFIDENCE

Ignorance... there's no confidence to equal it.
—Orson Welles

CHASE'S FALL

Chase Friedman had no idea that a single fateful decision to follow an attractive young woman back to her apartment would change his life forever. Chase's friends had convinced him to make the trip from his home in Los Angeles to Philadelphia for New Year's 2021—this was mid-COVID, so not a simple decision, even for a carefree twenty-five-year-old. But his friends said that they had already had COVID, so he would be safe. After the clock struck midnight, Chase accompanied the young woman and two of her friends back to her Philadelphia apartment. They "continued the party" at her place into the early hours of January 1. After a bit of sleep, Chase groggily stumbled into the bathroom, fell, and broke his neck.

In an instant, Chase found himself on a stranger's bathroom floor, a quadriplegic.

"I remember thinking I'm just gonna be a head the rest of my life, and I just wanted to die," Chase recalled two years later.

Rolling into surgery on January 2, Chase made eye contact with the anesthesiologist and thought, *I hope you have no idea what you're doing. I hope you are the worst anesthesiologist ever and you just let me fall asleep forever.* But Chase did wake up after surgery. Through a postoperative groggy haze, the doctors provided Chase a nebulous prognosis: "There's a chance you stay like this . . . [and] there's a chance you make some recovery." Clearly, the doctors didn't want to get too specific, but the cruel truth is that few people ever walk after an injury like Chase's, and many never regain the ability to feed themselves.[58]

The doctors added that to regain the most function, Chase needed to focus on two things: 1) work as hard as he could in rehab and 2) stay incredibly positive. But how could anyone stay positive in Chase's predicament?

Yet, Chase did notice the slightest bit of function in his left bicep that wasn't there before the surgery—something to be positive about. At that moment, a switch flipped inside him. With that glimmer of hope, Chase decided he was going to be the "Michael Jordan of spinal cord rehab."

Before the accident, Chase had never been the Michael Jordan of anything. He'd always been a good student "but never won any awards" and was a very good tennis player—good enough to play for a division III college team. But he'd never really played to his potential. "If I would've pushed myself one-hundred-percent, I probably could have been the number-one player on the team." Chase didn't push himself. He hadn't done the extra practices or workouts that the top players did. In fact, during his first twenty-five years, Chase had been satisfied with being "pretty good."

Yet a combination of that tingle in his bicep and the instructions from the doctors to "rehab hard" and "stay positive" changed Chase from someone who wanted to die only hours before to someone who would make a miraculous recovery.

DECEPTIVELY POSITIVE

One answer to the question posed at the beginning of this book—"How does a self-doubting person become confident?"—is a second well-meaning but somewhat unhelpful piece of advice: "Stay positive." Of course, if you have a positive outlook, you're more likely to be confident in your ability to get through the Bumpy Part of the learning curve or overcome an obstacle. But how does a quadriplegic, suddenly cut down in the prime of his life 2,700 miles from the support system of his family and friends, stay positive? Perhaps we can learn from Chase's extraordinary situation and apply his strategies to our own struggles with careers, obstacles, or skills we want to improve on.

Chase had a history of strange behavior when faced with dire situations. While in college, one of his best friends tragically and unexpectedly died of a fatal interaction between an epilepsy medicine and a recreational drug. "I remember everyone was freaking out, crying because this kid had died. But I said, 'He's not dead. This is a mistake.'" Chase was in complete denial. He went so far as to walk to his friend's house, where the ambulances were still flashing, and tried to get in. "Just let me talk to him." It took him a full day to come to terms with reality. Reflecting on it later, he said, "I had lost my mind."

While that episode from his college days doesn't sound emotionally healthy, Chase's tendency toward self-deception around bad news turned out to be surprisingly beneficial when it came to his spinal cord injury. For example, Chase did not want to hear about his prognosis or what his possible ceiling might be as far as physical capability. He didn't want to hear about other patients either. "I didn't Google my injury one time. When I was an inpatient, I didn't talk to any other patients because I didn't want to compare myself to them. I didn't want them to compare themselves to me. I just wanted to compare me to me." Chase had tapped into what Jason Lopez, a philosophy researcher, and Matthew Fuxjager, a physiology researcher, labeled the adaptive value of self-deception.[59]

Lopez and Fuxjager asked, "If tracking the truth is important for human survival and reproduction, then why is self-deception, a process that obscures the truth, so pervasive in human behavior?" We hear about negative examples of self-deception frequently: the alcoholic convinced they're able to stop drinking at any time, the gambler's confidence in winning back all their losses, or the narcissist overestimating their talent and intelligence despite average abilities. The research concludes that in certain contexts, positive self-deception has been shown to lead to better performance, particularly around competition and athletics.

The positive self-deception of positive self-talk before competition or public speaking has been shown in multiple studies to improve performance outcomes.[60] While the context is somewhat different, Chase would argue that his miraculous recovery was in part due to this self-deception against a lot of real-world evidence—the hesitancy and haziness of the doctors and his slow progress right after surgery when much of his movement was simply the physical therapists moving his body around. Yet, he said, "I saw myself making a completely full recovery. I just thought I was gonna be totally fine."

Chase's tendency toward self-deception manifested as positive vibes throughout rehab. Chase would celebrate every micro improvement, any tiny bit of extra range of motion compared to the previous day. "If something would change a little bit, I'm like, 'Win! That's a win!'" When he was first able to handle the most basic physical feat most of us take for granted, simply using his core muscles to hold himself up on the side of the bed, he hyped, "I'm a beast!" Even when there were bad days of no progress or regression, Chase found ways to keep his spirits high.

Serendipitously, one of his college tennis teammates became a spinal cord physician, often advising Chase about recovery. "He told me that this injury is like playing tennis, where some days you're playing amazing and other days you get out there and play like shit. You don't know what's going wrong. But the important thing to do is the next day, forget. And that's exactly what I did." Forgetting about the last play is a form of self-deception that many athletes use to come back from underwhelming performances, whether the previous day or the previous missed shot in basketball.

Former Golden State Warrior future Hall of Fame shooting guard Klay Thompson tore his ACL against the Toronto Raptors in the 2019 NBA Finals. The first time Thompson faced the Raptors at home after a grueling two-year recovery from the ACL and another serious leg injury, he started off terribly, missing his first five three-point shots in a row. Was he "in his head," thinking about the previous bad play? Not Klay Thompson. From that point forward, Klay made six of his next nine three-point attempts and finished with twenty-nine points to help the Warriors defeat the Raptors that night. After the game, teammate Steph Curry was asked about Klay's famous short-term memory. "He's the human goldfish. Dory from *Finding Nemo*, that's Klay. We love it. Just keep swimming."* What Steph meant was that Klay has complete confidence in his overall shooting ability. It doesn't matter if he missed the last shot, Thompson knows he's a great shooter and will not hesitate on the next opportunity. Forgetting about previous setbacks is another powerful form of self-deception and a way to stay positive in even the most dire circumstances.

BUILDING CONFIDENCE THROUGH EXPERIENCE

While maintaining a positive attitude, even in a self-deceptive way, is one powerful approach to maintaining confidence, a newbie at anything generally isn't confident at that skill. How do you build confidence in the first place? Arguably, the only way to initially build confidence in a skill is to "just do it." A common metaphor is "throw them into the deep end"—but how do you keep from drowning?

---

* Sorry, Steph. It's well documented that fish do not really have only short-term memories. But it's a useful metaphor, nonetheless. https://www.theage.com.au/national/schoolboy-explodes-goldfish-memory-myth-20080218-ge6qq7.html

Jason threw himself into the deep end of the real estate business by entrenching himself in Brian's office for up to thirty hours a week while still going to school full-time. Brian and Jason spent a little time talking about real estate basics. Then the process quickly turned hands-on, with Jason listening in on dozens of Brian's calls involving sellers and investors. These calls exposed Jason to techniques for building relationships, answering difficult questions, and closing deals. Pretty quickly, Brian encouraged Jason to make his own real estate calls—at first, with Brian listening in and then later on his own. Brian's approach to helping Jason by teaching him the foundational concepts, demonstrating, and quickly letting Jason actually experience the process of bringing together real estate transactions works well for most people in most circumstances. That is, the fastest way to build confidence on the Bumpy Part of the learning curve is to skim through the basics and just start executing the task, mistakes and all.

Jason's experience echoes this sentiment: "I cannot learn unless I am actually doing the thing. Even though you can sit here for an hour and tell me how to sell a property, I will never know how to do it unless I'm actually physically doing it. That's why I hated the classroom so much because none of it was doing." Even Jeremy, who dedicated his career to the education system, recognizes that deep learning only comes with taking action: "There's this idea of . . . you read a lot about it, you talk to people about it, and that's good. But I think until you try it, you don't bake it into your muscle memory in this deep way." Helen felt the same way: "A lot of the time, you learn stuff by doing it. And it's only through having a go that you realize, yeah, that worked, or no, that didn't work. Taking all that information and thinking that through is the data you can use to go forward."

Jason, Jeremy, and Helen are not alone in their preference for learning and building confidence by doing. Education theorists call this experiential learning. Experiential learning makes intuitive sense in many learning contexts. Think about the bike riding example at the beginning of the book. Imagine if every six-year-old had to sit in a classroom with twenty or so other bike learners, and a teacher guided them through a six-week course from a textbook approved by the school district on the proper methodology and safety techniques for riding a bike. Common sense says that wouldn't be a good approach for six-year-olds, but we don't have to rely on common sense. Academic researchers have been studying and validating the value of experiential learning for decades. One meta-analysis, *Experiential Learning—What Do We Know?*,[61] that covered sixteen studies conducted over forty years, examining over 1,000 subjects, concluded that "the use of experiential learning activities has a positive, significant effect on student learning and the student's perception of learning."

So, to build confidence on the Bumpy Part of a learning curve, you just "do it"? It's not quite that easy. First, many of these studies show that starting with a baseline of knowledge using traditional methods can accelerate experiential learning (think biology lecture followed by biology lab). This jibes with Jason's experience learning the real estate business. Before he just "did it," Jason embedded himself in Brian's office for a few months. Only after that baseline of knowledge was set did he even start talking to sellers and investors, and it took six months to get his first sale, which, of course, was another round of learning. Second, before you "just do it," there's some nuance on *how*. Researchers have found that there are multiple types of experiential learners. Your experiential learning type will affect how you approach a learning curve.

WHAT KIND OF EXPERIENTIAL LEARNER ARE YOU?

According to decades of research by education theorist David Kolb,[62] *all* learning is experiential. Kolb's definition of learning is to truly internalize something. For example, a child whose parent says, "Don't touch the stove, you could get burned" has some level of understanding that stoves are hot and could cause something called "burned." However, only when the child touches the stove and experiences a burn does that child internalize the knowledge of being careful around hot stoves. Kolb suggests all true learning is experiential, whether it's physical, like burning your hand on a stove, social, like understanding your audience for a presentation, or abstract, like how the Pythagorean theorem works. Kolb has labeled four progressive steps humans follow to turn an experience into internalized learning. *How* a person processes these four steps is indicative of their learning style. Once you're cognizant of your learning style, it's possible to improve the way you learn. To start, Kolb's four stages of turning an experience into learning are the following:

- **Doing**. You actively experience something firsthand. For example, a child touches a hot stove and feels pain.

- **Reviewing**. You reflect on your concrete experience and interpret what happened. For example, the child tries to figure out what caused all that pain.

- **Concluding**. You analyze your observations and come up with theories, concepts, or models to explain the experience. The child may generalize that stoves can cause pain.

- **Experimenting**. You apply and test what you learned in new situations to see if your conclusions work. The next time the child is near a stove, they are cautious and (if adventurous) touch it quickly or touch different parts to see which parts are hot versus not.

By cycling through these stages, people turn direct experiences into useful knowledge. Going back to Jason's frustration with classroom learning, classic lecture-style learning doesn't even hit the first phase of the experiential learning process. Essentially, classroom learning is equivalent to the parent's admonition: "Don't touch the stove. You could get burned." As we saw, the child didn't "learn" anything from that admonition. For centuries, billions of students have memorized facts and regurgitated them back on tests, but according to Kolb, true learning only happens if the learner progresses through the four steps the child went through in the stove-burning example.

Further, Kolb's research shows that different people are more comfortable with different stages of the experiential learning process, and these biases define four different learning styles.* According to Kolb, each of the four learning styles is defined by a person's preference for two of the four learning stages. Learning in the context of your dominant two stages allows you to learn most naturally and comfortably. The definitions below describe each learning style's preferences and weaknesses.

- **Experiencing**-style learners prefer to gather information through *doing* and *reviewing*. They learn at the ideation stage and are good at brainstorming ideas. They may be overly imaginative and emotional and struggle with practical applications.

- **Reflecting**-style learners are most comfortable *reviewing* and *concluding*, that is, thinking through ideas and building theoretical or abstract models. They learn best by reflecting and observing. They may focus too much on abstract concepts and struggle to act decisively.

- **Thinking**-style learners are oriented toward the practical application of ideas and problem-solving. They prefer learning through *concluding* and *experimenting* or applying concrete concepts to theoretical or abstract models. They can ignore interpersonal issues and may rush to find one correct answer rather than considering multiple options.

---

* I found Kolb's original four learning styles easier to understand and effective for the purposes of this book. However, more recently, he sliced and diced them into nine different learning styles. You can find out about all nine in *How You Learn Is How You Live: Using Nine Ways of Learning to Transform Your Life*.

- **Acting**-style learners enjoy carrying out plans and experiments involving new experiences, *experimenting* and *doing*. They tend to be intuitive and action-focused. They may rely too heavily on intuition rather than logic and avoid reflection, so they may rush from one experience to the next.

Again, these are not strict categories. For example, acting-style learners *can* use reflecting-style stages: *reviewing* and *concluding*. That's just not how they prefer to learn or their comfort zone. As we'll see, stretching yourself into another learning style has important benefits.

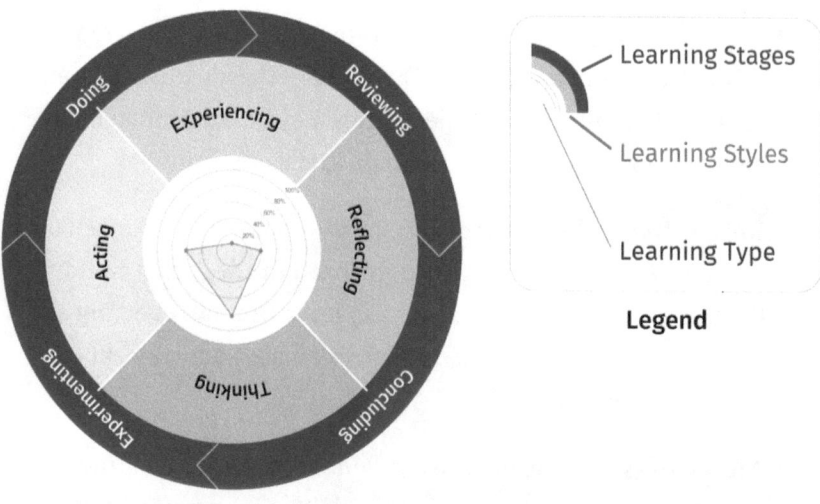

Figure 6—Kolb's Learning Stages and Styles

Above is a graphic that visually describes the relationship between learning stages and learning styles and adds one more element in the center—my own learning style as derived from taking the Kolb Experiential Learning Profile (KELP) assessment (which set me back $35).[63] Similar to the "Big Five" personality test assessment, the answers to these assessment questions can be difficult to answer definitively. The structure of each question requires the test taker to prioritize four different endings to a sentence like "When I learn..." In the sample question below, I liked all four answers, and I could argue all four of these answers are "True" for myself.

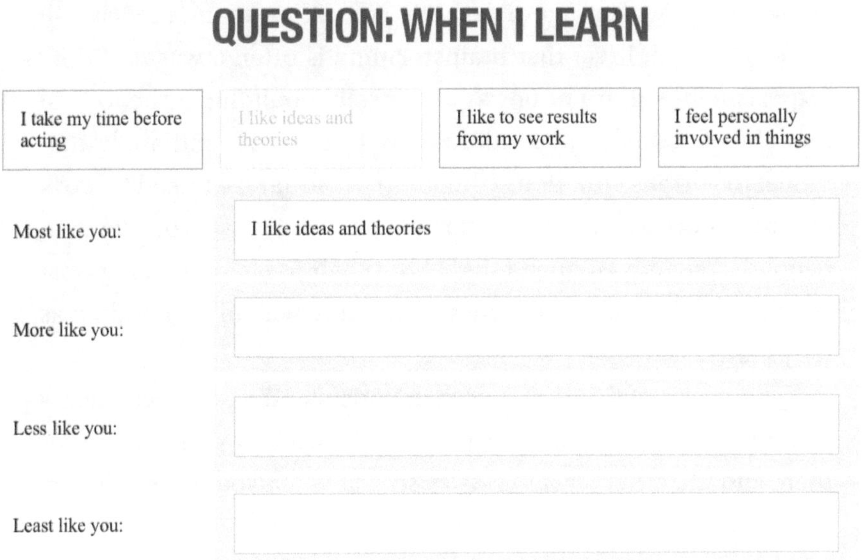

QUESTION: WHEN I LEARN

| I take my time before acting | I like ideas and theories | I like to see results from my work | I feel personally involved in things |

Most like you: I like ideas and theories

More like you:

Less like you:

Least like you:

Figure 7—Sample KELP 4.0 Question

So, prioritizing them was difficult and could yield different answers depending on recent activity or how I'm feeling. That said, given that there are twenty questions, often getting at the same point from various angles, I think the test did successfully identify my learning style.

Looking back to figure 6 above, there is a kite shape in the center of the white part of the circular graphic, indicating my personal biases on each of the four learning styles compared to Kolb's "normative sample" group of over 26,000 individuals. At the time I took this test, my learning style was biased most strongly toward *thinking* at around the eightieth percentile and second to acting at about the sixtieth percentile, whereas I was biased strongly away from the experience style. These results match well with my perception of myself. That is, I move from experiencing something new to truly understanding a topic best through deep involvement in and application of abstract ideas, theories, and concepts. I also enjoy fitting a wide range of data into concise ideas and models. On the other hand, I feel that brainstorming is often a waste of time (experiencing), and I'm not as comfortable building a theoretical model (reflecting), but I will happily test, verify, and apply that model to various situations (thinking). As for areas I need to work on, the report describes my learning challenges as "working with people," "keeping an open mind about their ideas," and being "lost in thought." I'm sure colleagues and family will all be nodding as they read this.

The power of this tool is both in understanding the weaknesses of your learning style so that you can consciously compensate for them and the other learning styles so that when you hit the Bumpy Part of the learning curve, you can ask yourself whether you're too much in your comfort zone and experiment with flexing to other, less comfortable learning styles. According to Kolb and his collaborators, when people are aware of their learning style and actively try to get out of their comfort zone, they become better learners, as shown by a Georgia State study of technology entrepreneurs, which found that learning flexibility positively affected innovation.[64] Interestingly, the more flexible learners were slower in making strategic decisions, but this process led to greater innovation. The authors surmised that taking more time with decisions allows flexible learners to better utilize all their learning capabilities, leading to more creativity and innovation compared to rigid style preferences.

Building confidence via an academic theory and an assessment test is not aligned with my thinking learning style. That said, after learning about Kolb's theory and being made aware of my own learning style (with all its strengths and weaknesses), I've gone out of my way to change my behavior in learning situations. For example, as a thinking-style learner, I have tried to be more open to people's ideas and reflect on them more thoroughly rather than prematurely dismissing them as unproven, which had been my tendency. This has led to uncomfortable brain stretching when I attempt to flex to a different learning style, which is always a good sign.

DELIBERATE PRACTICE FOR THE REST OF US

We've learned that being a flexible experiential learner can be a powerful tool in helping you gain confidence in building a skill. Of course, a critical component of experiential learning is simply practicing that skill. "Practice" is another answer to "How does a self-doubting person gain confidence?" This seems obvious, but there are some generalizable rules of practice to help people build confidence faster and more effectively.

As mentioned in the introduction, an often cited technique world-class performers use is a special form of practice called "deliberate practice." World-class performers use deliberate practice to progressively advance on the World Class Flat to compete with the best at that skill. However, the benefits of deliberate practice can also be a powerful tool to get through the Bumpy Part of the learning curve. So it's worth understanding what deliberate practice is and how we regular people can take advantage of it to improve a particular skill or achieve a goal and subsequently build confidence in ourselves.

Deliberate practice stretches the learner to improve a particular skill. The key elements of deliberate practice are

1. **An ambitious, measurable goal.** For example, achieving a perfect score on a standardized test, winning a particular tournament, or making 90 percent of your free throws. If the goal

is not measurable (e.g., "get better at crafting"), it's impossible to follow through on the rest of the deliberate practice elements.

2. **Maintain focus.** When practicing anything, it can be easy to mindlessly repeat the same activity and call it "practice." For example, shooting baskets at a local park for thirty minutes may be fun, but that activity is unlikely to make you incrementally better at shooting. Someone using deliberate practice would use that same thirty minutes to focus on the goal (say, making 50 percent of three-point shots) and concentrate and reflect on every shot. With each attempt, they would evaluate what went well and what didn't and focus on micro improvements for the next shot (e.g., How much arc did the ball have? How did the ball come off my fingers? What was the position of my elbow?). Mindlessly practicing any skill reinforces old habits. Deliberate practice with focus creates new positive habits.

3. **Constant feedback.** An important component of deliberate practice is getting constant feedback from an external, objective observer who's skilled in coaching or mentoring this skill. This person will help you find and correct errors and refine techniques that would be impossible to do on your own.

4. **Practicing out of your comfort zone.** To improve on any skill, you must take on challenges that go beyond your current skill level. For example, learning a piece of music that's much more difficult to play than you're used to or volunteering for a task at work you haven't done before. If you do the same thing repeatedly, getting significantly better is impossible. Deliberate practice requires stretching.

5. **Repetition.** You have to practice regularly and often. By practicing the refined techniques over and over again, those newly refined skills can get to an "autopilot" stage so that you can move on to learning other, even more difficult aspects of the skill. A not fully

agreed upon sub-point to this repetition element is that to become world-class at something, you must invest at least 10,000 hours of practice time in it—the so-called "10,000 hours rule."

6. **Self-motivation.** As discussed earlier, if you're not intrinsically motivated to get better, it's extremely hard to improve. Your practice activity should be powered by an internal drive to improve versus a push from an external source like parents or peers.

How do these rules of deliberate practice differ for people on the Bumpy Part of the learning curve versus those on the World Class Flat? The recommendations are largely the same with the biggest differences around elements 1 and 5. The goal must still be measurable, but it is likely to be less ambitious than world-class. And that's okay because the time investment described in element 5, repetition, is unlikely to be close to the controversial 10,000 hours—but something much less. Back to the tenets of the book, learning a skill to proficiency gives you the choice to move on to other skills or continue to improve on that skill.

I didn't realize it at the time, but I used these deliberate practice techniques to reach proficiency with a somewhat frivolous but fun life skill: bowling. When I was a fifth grader, the local bowling alley organized a league for Saturday mornings that I got swept into while trying to be more social. I participated for two years but never improved—I was happy to break 100 each game and was more interested in trying to figure out sixth-grade girls than improving my bowling skills.

Decades later, a different local bowling alley 2,500 miles away offered all the students in my twin sons' elementary school a single, free game of bowling every day, all summer. My nine-year-old boys had nothing to do, so every day, they'd get their free bowling game card punched, put on those stinky rented bowling shoes, and throw the beat-up house balls down the lane. They had fun every day and looked forward to the bowling alley's video game machines and junk food as much as the bowling. After a few weeks, the staff noticed them coming every day and invited the boys to join the fall youth bowling league. As soon as competition was involved, this playful activity suddenly became much more serious. In a relatively short amount of time, we bought each boy custom bowling balls, bowling shoes, and various other accoutrements and eventually hired a bowling coach. At this point, I was still bowling around 100 every game, using my weak-wristed sixth-grade technique, and these fourth graders had wonderful form, were using sophisticated "hook" shots, and averaged 160 or better. Both boys commonly rolled 200 in games. That's when my need for deliberate practice kicked in.

My *goal* was to get good enough at bowling to participate in a father-son league and not embarrass myself or my children. In all the other father-son teams in this age group, the father was a better bowler than the son. So my goal was to at least match my sons' bowling capabilities, which were clearly out of my *comfort zone*. My form of *feedback* was to leverage my sons' coach to get pointers and techniques. Heck, I was paying him, so I just started bowling during their sessions, asking questions, and getting pointers. In addition, my sons had much more knowledge about the sport than I did and provided me with lots of corrective techniques. I was fortunate at the time to work for a company that shut down for two weeks over the year-end holidays. So I took that block of time to go bowling *every single day* with my sons for two consecutive weeks (*repetition*). And my *motivation*? I didn't just want to get better for my sons; I wanted to get better for myself—I was motivated to enjoy this skill the rest of my life. During those final two weeks of the year, I worked through a few Bumpy hurdles, hit the inflection point, and something clicked. I had jumped up the steepest part of the bowling learning curve. By the New Year, I had already bowled a few 200 games and felt ready to join the father-son league that started in January. In the league,

I ended up averaging a respectable 170 and was just fine with that. Will I ever join the senior bowling tour or even bowl in a league without my sons? Nope. But whenever there happens to be a bowling outing at work or with friends, I step out on the lanes with a lot of confidence and have more fun than I used to.

EVERY SINGLE DAY

I can't overstate the value of practicing every day while on the Bumpy Part of the bowling learning curve. Chase intuitively felt the importance of daily progress as well. His physical therapists were supposed to be off on the weekends. However, "Every single day seems to make a big difference. I needed someone to come in and stretch me out [on the weekends]. I needed someone to come in and just do extra work with me." So Chase convinced one or two physical therapists to come in for just an hour or so on the weekends to maintain his rehabilitation activity. In his tennis playing days, Chase was not the guy doing the extra workouts or practices, but the self-crowned Michael Jordan of spinal cord rehab needed the extra weekend physical therapy sessions. Later, after getting out of the rehab hospital, Chase bought a treadmill for his apartment in San Diego. "I was on the treadmill every single day for as long as I could because the best way to get better at walking is to walk."

Similarly, during her critical awakening moment, when Helen Wells rediscovered her passion for art after breaking up with her boyfriend, she went to the Slade School of Art studio every day for two weeks. In addition, when I consulted the literature for advice on book writing for novices like me, the most frequently cited tenet was "write every day."

Given that writers are told to write every day, athletes are coached to practice every day. Language learners are taught to speak their target language every day. What is it about doing something every day that improves learning and performance? Might the old night-before-cram session actually perform better? What about spreading out the learning, practicing, or creating with longer intervals like every few days or once a week?

Part of the answer lies in how learning at spaced intervals[65] can improve the ability of your brain to build and retain memories. Learning something new causes molecular changes in the brain, strengthening connections between neurons representing that memory.* The process of consolidating and stabilizing these changes so that memory is stored long-term is called memory consolidation, which involves the new growth of synapses and proteins. When a memory is recalled (such as when you're practicing a skill), it goes through reconsolidation, where the memory traces are temporarily destabilized and then restabilized by similar molecular processes, thereby strengthening the memory.

What scientists have theorized and shown in various studies and research going as far back as 1885[66] is that when this recall or practice happens at *spaced intervals*, memory recall is better. That is, being pounded repeatedly with the same material without time to process that information yields worse learning performance than when allowing for time between learning sessions. Importantly, the learning interval (the time between learning sessions), as compared to learning performance, follows an inverted U-shaped curve with a notable step up at twenty-four hours.[67] If the interval is too short, there's not enough time to process the memory; if it's too long, the memory is forgotten. Starting at around the twenty-four-hour interval, the recall performance gets much better. The significance of twenty-four hours appears to be driven by what happens during sleep.

• • •

---

* Note that memory has a broader meaning in this context than just "declarative memory" or facts and figures. It also includes, among other things, 1) procedural memory, for example, remembering procedures and skills like riding a bike, 2) episodic memory, the autobiographical memories of your life events, and 3) spatial memory, remembering relationships between objects in space for navigation and where you put your keys.

In Matthew Walker's 2017 bestseller *Why We Sleep: Unlocking the Power of Sleep and Dreams*,[68] he recounts the story of a pianist struggling with a difficult piece of music that he couldn't play fluently despite trying countless times in a row. The pianist went to bed in frustration, but when he woke up the next morning, he played the piece flawlessly. This story started Walker on his journey to understand how closely related sleep is to learning. Walker's subsequent research uncovered that, during sleep, memories are reactivated and reconsolidated, as described above, even without physically practicing anything. Slow-wave sleep, also known as "deep sleep," is particularly important to forming these consolidated memories. So, the twenty-four-hour interval is important because you can improve your skill level by simply getting a good night's sleep. Practicing more frequently during the day doesn't afford this special nighttime processing, and practicing less frequently can lead to those memories deteriorating before they can be reinforced by the next day's practice. Hence, doing something daily builds on the skill from one day to the next and helps solidify yesterday's learnings without you doing anything!

In addition, doing something daily can turn an activity into a habit, particularly if performed at either the same time, place, or both every day.[69] It seems the popular culture "three-week rule" (if you do an activity daily for three consecutive weeks, you'll turn it into a habit) is essentially an unsubstantiated observation by plastic surgeon (right, not psychologist or neuroscientist) Maxwell Maltz in his 1960 book *Psycho-Cybernetics*.[70] More recent controlled studies indicate that, depending on the particular habit (say, flossing), habit formation can take fifty-nine days or even longer.[71] But the good news is that daily practice *can* form habits, which means building confidence in a skill requires less of a conscious effort. Doing it daily makes it easier to stick with the program.

• • •

How long can people keep practicing and improving every single day? As someone who attempted to follow my own advice to write this book, I blocked out two two-hour sessions each day, including weekends, to write. I updated my calendar entries to repeat "forever." For me, waking up and writing first thing in the morning caught my brain in its most alert state. After two or three hours, I stopped writing to work on other projects, exercise, eat lunch, and take a twenty- to thirty-minute power nap midafternoon. I found that a nap refreshed my brain enough so I could intensely focus on writing again for another couple of hours. Even with this relatively easy schedule (as compared to my startup days), I couldn't keep it up for more than three weeks without my writing productivity falling off.

I discovered the value of rest days when I was forced to take time off because of travel, sickness, or other life events that got in the way. At first, I was disappointed in myself for not being able to follow my own advice about practicing every day.* Then I found that, while it often took a day or two to ramp up after one of these breaks, the short recess rejuvenated me, and I was able to get back into my daily three- to four-hour writing routine for another few weeks. So, I started digging into this ubiquitous "write every day" mantra. Is it true? Could regular people actually do this? For how long? And did it help?

During media interviews, prolific author Stephen King often professes that he "writes every day except for Christmas, the Fourth of July, and my birthday." But in his book *On Writing: A Memoir of the Craft*, he admitted that was a lie. When he was writing, he actually wrote every single day, including Christmas, the Fourth, and his birthday. He just didn't want to sound like a "workaholic dweeb" to interviewers.

So it seems at least some world-class people like Stephen King

---

* Accomplishing a big, long-term task like writing a book is clearly different from learning a new skill, though both benefit and have research around this every day concept.

can do this every day thing for a long, long time. But what about us regular people? University of Auckland education researcher Helen Sword helped answer some of these questions in her 2016 academic article, "'Write Every Day!': a Mantra Dismantled."[72]

Sword found that those who supported the *write every day* mantra usually turned to behavioral psychologist Robert Boice's research documented in his 1990 book *Professors as Writers: A Self-Help Guide to Productive Writing*.[73] Boice ran a series of experiments showing that those who wrote in brief, daily sessions were far more productive than those who wrote in large blocks of time. However, Sword looked more closely at the research and found that Boice's sample sizes were way too small for statistical significance (in one case, nine subjects split into three groups), and the strict writing regimens were enforced under artificial conditions. Famously, if participants in the write-every-day cohort missed a day of writing, they were forced to contribute money to a hated organization. Sword went on to do her own research, including a survey of over 1,200 academic writers, and found that only 11.5 percent of them reported that they write, or at least aspire to write, every day. In follow-up interviews, Sword found that successful writing approaches varied wildly. Some people wrote every weekday while others took long breaks and sequestered themselves for months at a time.

What's the takeaway? The power of daily practice, coupled with the memory-enhancing benefits of sleep, can elevate your learning and performance. Unless you're superhuman like Stephen King, incorporating break days is necessary and will recharge you to go on another dedicated productivity streak. If you can strike the right balance between daily effort and restorative breaks, you'll be amazed at the transformative results you can achieve. But you may need the power of ignorance to get even farther.

IGNORANCE

By twenty-six, Orson Welles was already an accomplished theater actor, director, and producer, on and off Broadway. However, he had absolutely no filmmaking experience—not acting, not cinematography, not film production. On his first try at filmmaking, he created one of the most legendary movies of all time: *Citizen Kane*.

How could a complete neophyte make one of the greatest films ever made? Nearly two decades after the film was released, a curious BBC interviewer[74] asked where Welles found the confidence to try such a thing. Welles responded, "Ignorance, sheer ignorance. There's no confidence to equal it. It's only when you know something about a profession that you are timid or careful." When asked to elaborate, Welles went on to say, "I thought you could do anything with a camera that the eye could do . . . and if you come up from the bottom in the film business, you're taught all the things that the cameraman doesn't want to attempt, for fear he will be criticized for having failed . . . [but] I didn't know that there were things you couldn't do. So anything I could think of in my dreams, I attempted to photograph."

With fearlessness fueled by ignorance, Welles innovated foundational film techniques, including deep focus cinematography,[75] an approach no film veteran had conceived of at the time.

The recommendation isn't to simply jump in and attempt to operate at the highest levels of skill when you have no experience in it. In fact, a well-known cognitive bias called the Dunning-Kruger effect suggests the opposite—people with limited competence in a particular domain often overestimate their abilities and get into trouble with overconfidence. However, looking deeper into Orson Welles's case with *Citizen Kane* is instructive. While ignorant of film production, Welles attracted some of the top talent in the film industry to support him. In that same interview, Welles went on to say, "I had a great advantage not only in the real genius of my cameraman [famed cinematographer Gregg Toland] but in the fact that he . . . told me . . . there was nothing about camera work that . . . any intelligent person couldn't learn in half a day."

BUT HE'S ORSON WELLES. CAN I DO THAT?

Outsmart the Learning Curve is for and about "regular" people. While Orson Welles is quite an exception, applying this concept to people like you and me is well within reach. Armed with ignorance and circumstance, I've found success in domains that I had no business entering. For example, Palm hired me in 1993 as a software product manager because, at that moment, it *was* a software company.

Then Palm's founders decided the only way the company could survive was to pivot to hardware.[76] While many other Palm employees had worked at hardware companies like Apple, Grid, and Radius, I didn't know the first thing about hardware design or production. I was such a software-oriented person; at the time, I couldn't describe the difference between mechanical and industrial engineering. I started slowly, only taking on software aspects of the original Palm Pilot. But as Palm grew quickly, I ended up leading the most complex piece of hardware we had on the roadmap: the first handheld wireless device eventually called the Palm VII. How did I come up to speed?

Simply by being unafraid to ask lots of naive questions and learning from my peers. Similar to Orson Welles, my stellar and helpful Palm colleagues served as my guardrails and convinced me that hardware wasn't that intimidating. One electrical engineering friend claimed his electrical engineering job was the easiest in the world because all he did was "shop in a catalog and wire the parts together." I'm certain I couldn't learn what that engineer knows "in half a day," but I'm thankful that he and many other hardware engineers taught me enough to make informed decisions and were open enough to let me make significant contributions.

DO REALITY DISTORTION FIELDS WORK?

After getting up to speed on wireless hardware on Palm VII and later on some of the first successful smartphones,[77] *I* became one of those experts who knew "too much." I had lost the powerful ignorance that enabled confidence in innovative ideas. I remember being amazed when I first heard that the original iPhone integrated cellular, Wi-Fi, and Bluetooth wireless technology, all in an incredibly compact form factor.

Knowing too much about how difficult it is to integrate a single wireless radio into a small form factor, the idea of integrating *three* wireless technologies in one device would have sounded like an "impossible" project—one that I would have labeled too risky at the time.

Implementing the insanely risky specs of the original iPhone required a very special form of ignorance—Steve Jobs's reality distortion field.[78] Jobs could famously convince team members that any impossible task was, in fact, possible. I can only imagine the depths of the reality distortion field required to persuade the team that integrating all these technologies into one small, beautiful form factor was possible.

STEPS TO ENTERING A NEW DOMAIN

What are the takeaways from the stories of Orson Welles and Steve Jobs, not to mention my own humble story? If you're curious about entering a new domain, here are a few simple steps to take on the challenge:

1. **Embrace the beginner's mindset.** Don't let a lack of knowledge or experience in the new domain intimidate you.

2. **Find experts** who can provide guidance. While you bring a fresh perspective, learning from domain experts can help you come up to speed faster and avoid pitfalls.

3. **Ask lots of questions,** even if they seem naive. Don't be afraid to ask fundamental questions about the new domain to learn from those with more experience. Most people are happy to share their knowledge.

4. **Recognize that most things are learnable.** An intelligent person can learn the fundamentals of many fields relatively quickly. Of course, it takes much longer to become a true expert, but coming up a basic learning curve enough to make important contributions can happen quickly.

MOST THINGS ARE FIGURE-OUT-ABLE

Soon after Helen had that surreal experience of hearing voices telling her to follow her path to art, she took the brave step of quitting her job at the nonprofit to become a full-time artist. She had saved about six months of living expenses, which she thought was a reasonable timeline to start making her living as an artist. Quitting her job was a bold move, but she was being careful about it. "I wanted to have a life where I create art and make my own living, [but] I had no clue how to do that."

She spent most of the first few months focusing on improving the quality of her art and coming up to speed on how she could turn art into a money-making venture. Like Orson Welles, she was a neophyte in the niche she was entering, but she wondered whether she had any transferable skills. So, she completed a personal "audit" of her business skills to figure out where the holes were. Doing this audit reassured her that she was not, in fact, starting from zero—she had done quite a bit of writing and marketing in her career, but she needed to work on several areas where she was weaker, particularly around building a social media presence. When I asked her how she was able to come up to speed on her weaker areas, she echoed Gregg Toland's words on learning camera work: "I fundamentally think that most things are figure-out-able . . . particularly with the internet. I didn't know how to build a website, but I learned how to build a website by looking at some YouTube videos." And when Helen was coming up to speed on her weak areas, there were no freely available AI chatbots. Today, with the support of various AI tools, most things are even more "figure-out-able."

While she was making progress in learning how to build a social presence, she hadn't made a penny on her art business, and the six-month deadline was approaching. So, by working her network, she reduced her financial risk with a part-time job that would "effectively pay all of my bills and allowed me to have four or five days doing what I love and finding a path." Helen's lesson: be fearless, but don't run out of money.

Months later, Helen's supportive but impatient husband said, "There's really no point in making loads of art and just having it under the bed where no one can see it." Helen literally had pieces under the bed because she had nowhere else to put them. Motivated by her husband's remark, Helen took digital photos of five pieces and put them on an online art shop to sell. Three of them sold in the first week! That started the business part of her journey and gave her the confidence that there was a way to monetize, which motivated her to find other avenues of earning. Not long after her first piece sold, Helen won an art competition, which provided social proof of her artistic capability. With that endorsement, she thought she might have a strong enough reputation to make some money teaching an art class. She wrote a little synopsis of the class contents and put it on all her social media platforms. The synopsis caught the attention of a book publisher, who contacted her and asked if she could turn that class into a book.

Once the book was published, Helen reached a point where she had multiple sources of income: selling original art, creating commissioned art, teaching classes, and selling books. This diversification strategy protected her in case one revenue stream fell off and created synergy through word-of-mouth and reputation-building that strengthened each source. Finally, she quit her part-time job. Helen completed her namesake Venn diagram and continues to dedicate her life to the thing she's loved since she was a little girl.

• • •

Helen didn't need a degree in marketing to jump-start her art business. By being fearless about most things being "figure-out-able," she was able to get the flywheel going without being a pure expert at any aspect of the business. I think there's often too much credence given to people with degrees (medicine, law, science, engineering) when actual knowledge and skill can be picked up so quickly, especially in today's internet and AI age. Said another way, not enough credit is given to experts in particular areas who don't have specific degrees. The 120 credits a person might have taken twenty years ago are likely irrelevant to what's happening now.

My story as an English major who later had a successful career in technical product management illustrates that self-taught people can succeed. Unlike many of my peers, I do not have a computer science or engineering degree. Yet somehow, I gained enough knowledge (and confidence) in product design, project management, and development to lead the definition and implementation of dozens of successful software and hardware products over my career.

As a kid, tinkering with computers was my hobby, similar to tinkering with cars for some of my friends. After taking one computer science class in high school, I convinced my father that I could program the billing system for his small businesses—talk about the Dunning-Kruger effect of overconfidence as a neophyte. My dad took his seventeen-year-old son's confidence as competence and bought a Radio Shack TRS-80 desktop computer with 8K of memory and a single floppy disk for storage to run a billing system for over 2,000 customers.

Just to be clear, this computer didn't have 8GB (billion) or 8MB (million); referred to as "Trash-80," it had only 8K (thousand) bytes to run the operating system, the development environment (Microsoft Basic), and my billing software. Note, too, that this was 1981—no off-the-shelf accounting software ran on a TRS-80. Similar functionality could only be found on giant mainframe computers at the time. Nor were there any foundational building block tools developers take for granted today to create, for example, user interfaces or support managing databases. This project was from scratch.

Halfway through the summer, I realized I had approached the problem in a completely unworkable way and needed more memory and storage to build a functional billing system. My confidence deflated, and I feared I couldn't come through on my promise to my father. So we upgraded the TRS-80 to a whopping 48K and added a second floppy disk drive. I pretty much started over, having learned what not to do. The fresh start and "tons" of memory were freeing, and I was able to code the whole thing from scratch in the final six weeks of the summer. I learned a few lessons from that project:

1. I started out completely ignorant of what it would take to build this system, with way too much confidence. I was in no position to develop something so complex that could potentially bring down my dad's business if it didn't work or broke down.

2. After initially failing, I was rightfully humbled and a bit scared that I might not be able to pull it off. But when my second attempt worked, that was empowering. It was perhaps the first time I realized that the best way to gain confidence in a skill is to simply do it—bumpiness and all.

3. After that summer and the following one, in which I coded the company's payroll system, I decided I didn't want to be a programmer. I couldn't imagine myself staring at a screen for eight hours a day for years on end (ha—look at me now).

Hence, I became an English major, not because I loved literature or writing but because I had no idea what I wanted to do with my life. I feared any math or science class outside of computer science. Brief hopes to transfer to the undergraduate business program were dashed with a D on a microeconomics final. So I held out for law school as an option—until I read Norman Mailer's *The Executioner's Song*, which exposed the nasty side of lawyering and turned me off to a legal career.

That said, I used the money I earned programming my dad's accounting systems to buy my first personal computer, an Osborne 1. This was a rare and expensive purchase at the time. It's hard to believe today, but I may have been the only person in my dorm freshman year who had their own computer. Computers were my hobby, after all, and that kept my glimmer burning. Maybe most valuable, though, is that I proved to myself that I didn't need a formal computer science education to code. I could come up a learning curve without a lot of classic training—just by trial and error and fighting through that discomfort of not knowing exactly how things would turn out. Compared to learning things like microeconomics in a lecture hall with 300 other students, coding and experiencing the failures and successes as I went was not only easier for me but empowering and eventually gave me the confidence to find my footing career-wise on the technology path.

IS EXTROVERSION A CHEAT CODE FOR LIFE?

In the "Openness" chapter, we learned about the Big Five personality traits, but we didn't get into much detail about the extroversion trait. Of course, extroversion is not the same as confidence, but extroverted people often *appear* to be confident, and that appearance of confidence seems to convey a lot of the same benefits as true confidence. It may be hard to believe, but solid academic research indicates that people high on the extroversion personality scale are happier,[79] perceived to be more intelligent,[80] more likely to find leadership roles,[81] and even luckier.

Richard Wiseman noted in *The Luck Factor* that those high on the extroversion scale are more likely to consider themselves lucky. Much of the luck seems to stem from extroverts being better networkers, leading to more connections and opportunities for serendipitously positive outcomes. This feels like we're working up to another one of those high school counselor motivational cliches: "Just be more outgoing." Can an introverted person become extroverted? That is, can introverts behave more extroverted, at least outwardly, to get some of the benefits enjoyed by people high on the extroversion scale? Further, can extroverts move even higher on the extroversion scale, especially if it can lead to better outcomes?

Amazingly, the answer to both questions is "yes."

A clever 2020 study out of the University of California, Riverside,[82] explored this question by splitting 131 college students into two groups. One group was asked to behave more extrovertedly for a week, while the other was asked to behave more introvertedly. The next week, the two groups switched.

This experimental setup was designed to determine whether there was a *causal* relationship between increased extroversion behavior and concrete outcomes. Note that most Big Five personality studies point to *correlative* results. If you're hazy on the causal/correlative stuff, causal studies show a direct relationship (e.g., smoking causes lung cancer), whereas correlative studies observe a relationship between two variables without proving causation (e.g., when ice-cream sales go up, shark attacks do too). While correlation is interesting, causal results are more enlightening and actionable.

The causal results of the UC-Riverside experiment were eye-opening. The researchers found that those *acting more extroverted* for a week had the following self-reported positive effects, independent of whether they participated as extroverts in the first or second week:

- **Higher positive affect**. Subjects reported substantially higher positive emotions (e.g., joy, excitement, enthusiasm).

- **Increased connectedness**. Subjects felt more connected with and close to others.

- **Improved flow**. Subjects reported higher levels of flow (feeling energized, focused, involved in activities).

- **Higher life satisfaction**. Subjects rated their overall life satisfaction more favorably.

- **Improved competence**. Subjects felt more competent and believed they could master hard challenges.

- **More autonomy**. Subjects felt more autonomous and freer to do things their own way.

The researchers found that each of these improvements had a substantial .2 to .3 standard deviations of difference between the introverted week and the extroverted week.

How did the researchers advise the subjects to be more extroverted for that week? They simply instructed the subjects to "try to act as talkative, assertive, and spontaneous as you can." To increase adherence to this advice, they also told the students that previous research found these behaviors beneficial for college students.

In addition, the researchers asked the participants to list five specific ways they planned to change their behavior over the next week. This exercise was intended to increase the impact of the instructions and has been shown in other research to be effective for this purpose. Last, the researchers sent three emails during the week to remind participants of their assigned behavior.

Beyond these simple instructions, the specific techniques and plans were completely left up to each participant. Note, too, that the researchers conducted a baseline Big Five personality test on the subjects, and their baseline results affected neither their outcomes nor which group they were assigned to. That is, no matter where they were on the extroversion scale at baseline, asking them to act more extroverted for a week yielded an increase in positive feelings.

Clearly, this is a limited study, with only college students, conducted over a two-week period. Much more study should be done to validate these findings. With those caveats, this study indicates that whether you're an introvert or an extrovert, simply consciously adopting more extroverted behaviors, such as being more talkative, assertive, and spontaneous, can have profound effects on your well-being, connectedness, and even competence.

So, no matter what your personality trait inclinations may be, challenge yourself to experiment with extroversion in your daily life. Try striking up a conversation with a colleague or sharing your ideas more assertively in a meeting. Pay attention to how these changes make you feel and the impact they have on your relationships and overall well-being. Perhaps the most empowering takeaway is that you can make positive improvements to your happiness, connectedness, and life satisfaction simply by being brave enough to "act" in an extroverted way.

PRACTICAL GUIDE/SUMMARY

- Positivity boosts performance and confidence. Even when it's hard to stay positive, take a lesson from Chase and many competitive athletes to stay positive in the face of daunting odds (self-deception). Don't let reality limit your goals.

- When on your journey across the Bumpy Part of the learning curve, forget about previous setbacks and envision your future success. Past history is not a predictor of future success.

- Seeking small wins builds confidence over time. Celebrate progress and micro-successes.

- Take the KELP assessment test to understand your learning style. Then, practice flexing to other styles when in a difficult learning situation.

- Leverage the power of deliberate practice to improve skills and build confidence. This means setting measurable goals, practicing outside your comfort zone, soliciting regular feedback from coaches or experts, and practicing consistently and often.

- Practice every day to overcome hurdles and build confidence. This might be a "sprint" of a week or two. If it's longer than that, include rest days to avoid burnout.

- Don't let inexperience stop you from gaining experience. Sometimes, coming into an area with a clean slate can give you an advantage. Steps to enter a new domain:

- Embrace the beginner's mindset.
- Find experts.
- Ask lots of questions.
- Recognize that most things are learnable (figure-out-able).
- Practice extroversion behaviors, such as being more talkative, assertive, and spontaneous, to gain the benefits of being an extrovert, even if you're an introvert.

For more extensive guidance and exercises to build confidence, check out the *Outsmart the Learning Curve* Workbook at https://www.outsmartbook.com/workbook or use the QR code below. It includes a simplified KELP assessment to get a baseline on your learning style.

CHAPTER 5
RESILIENCE

Many of life's failures are people who did not realize how close they were to success when they gave up.
—Thomas Edison

PREDICTING SUCCESS FROM FAILURE

When Jason was working for his real estate mentor, Brian, his first deal was getting tantalizingly close. He started working in Brian's office in March 2018, studied for the real estate license exam, and passed by the end of summer. Depending on his school schedule, to find his first client, he'd come in three to five times a week to use Brian's "archaic approach" to customer acquisition—cold-calling. Over months, he built contacts and relationships, but nothing turned into a transaction. Remember, he hadn't been paid a dime in nine months. "It was wearing on me." Finally, in November, he found a multifamily unit owner who selected Jason to be his agent to sell the property. To consummate the deal, they sat at a kitchen table to sign all the paperwork. The owner's son was taking the lead while his mother sat nervously at the table and his ill father lay in bed in the next room. Once the paperwork was signed, Jason was on top of the world. He'd finally gotten his first listing—the first is always the hardest.

Two days later, the son called to let Jason know that his father had died and that the building was not included in any will or trust. This meant that before the property could be sold, it would have to go through probate, a long and bureaucratic court process to sort out his father's assets. Of course, Jason felt horrible for his client and his family and was extremely compassionate about the situation. But when he hung up the phone, he thought, *I made a huge mistake.* The mistake wasn't spending time with this unlucky client; it was changing his entire career path and investing nine months of his life doing this real estate thing that didn't seem to be working out. He seriously considered quitting the next day, but "something in my gut told me to stick with it . . . that I've learned so much, and I'll figure it out."

In a speech to students at his alma mater, San Diego State, four years later, Jason told his audience of real estate wannabes, "Success and failure live really close to each other." What he meant is that you can try and fail many times over and not really know how close you are to success. Somebody might try and fail three times and quit, never knowing if the fourth attempt could have led to success. Jason was right at that line when his first deal blew up. If he had quit that day, he would have never known the unfathomable heights of success he'd reach just a few years later. How can anyone know whether they're at the precipice of success or doomed to continue to fail over and over again?

WHAT DO NIH RESEARCHERS AND TERRORISTS HAVE IN COMMON?

"If at first you don't succeed, try, try again." Is that true? How long should Jason have to keep trying . . . forever?

What if I told you that some math geniuses at Northwestern University published a paper[83] in *Nature* that derived a formula to determine whether an individual or group would eventually succeed or fail at something? While the model can't pinpoint the exact number of tries, the researchers uncovered the factors determining eventual success or terminal failure.

To prove their point had statistical significance, the researchers needed multiple large datasets of individuals or groups who made consecutive attempts at an objective that only sometimes led to success. In addition, the datasets needed to include some measure of improvement between failures and a clear definition of success. They wanted datasets from highly disparate domains to see if the models could be applied more broadly. The three datasets they used were

- **NIH grant seekers,** specifically those vying for the competitive R01 grants. Their measure of improvement was a percentile score the applicant received when the grant was denied, and success was defined as an application that resulted in the grant being awarded.

- **Entrepreneurs** who founded multiple ventures over time. Improvement was measured by total funds raised during each venture, and success was defined as either going public or selling the company at a high value within five years of the initial investment.

- **Terrorist organizations.** Yes, as insane as this sounds, the paper did not make any apologies or note any ethical considerations about selecting this controversial dataset. Worse, the measure of improvement for the terrorist groups was how many people were wounded in subsequent attacks, and success was defined as killing at least one person in an attack. Of course, terrorist organizations are horrible; however, if we can learn from their terrible actions, we should.

It would be hard to argue that these aren't disparate datasets, making the results even more compelling.

When the researchers boiled down all the advanced math and data analysis, they found two factors that were determinants of success across all three datasets. The first was simply the amount of time between attempts. If the time between attempts was shorter with each attempt, the likelihood of success increased. If no time-based pattern was observed between attempts, the model more likely predicted ultimate failure.

The researchers did not delve much into why reducing the time between attempts led to improved success rates, but "fail fast" is not a corporate mantra for nothing. When iterating more quickly, individuals or groups get more chances or trials. In most success or failure situations, there are tight windows of opportunity. If an individual or organization can't generate another attempt within that window, they may never succeed. Longer lag time leads to loss of insights gained from the previous failure. Successful individuals and groups incorporate learning from earlier failures, but taking too much time between failures mitigates the value of that learning—they forget. Last, shorter iterations also provide more data points to analyze and opportunities to try different variations.

The second determinant of success was the amount of improvement between attempts. Whether it be the NIH grant percentile score, the total funding for the next venture, or the number of people wounded in the next terrorist attack, substantial improvement between attempts was indicative of ultimate success. Negligible improvement between attempts predicted that an individual or group was unlikely to ever succeed at the task. In the case of the NIH grants, the success group showed, on average, a 6 percent increase in percentile scores between the first and second attempt, the entrepreneurs averaged a 20 percent increase in funding between the first and second venture, and the average "successful" terrorist increased casualty count by about 30 percent between the first and second attempt. It's notable that unsuccessful groups showed no statistically significant performance gains between attempts in any of the domains.

Tying together the first timing-based or temporal variable and the second variable measuring improvement, the researchers came up with a magic constant k, which, as they describe, "measure(s) the number of previous attempts one considers when formulating a new one." So, for example, in the NIH grant application case, the more parts of previous grant applications researchers can use (things they got right), the more they're likely to succeed. Essentially, k is a measure of how much learning and feedback people put into their subsequent attempts. The fascinating thing is when you plot out values for k, there is a clear area that the researchers called the *stagnation region*, which represents individuals or teams who "reject prior attempts and thrash around for new versions, not gaining enough feedback to initiate a pattern of intelligent improvements."

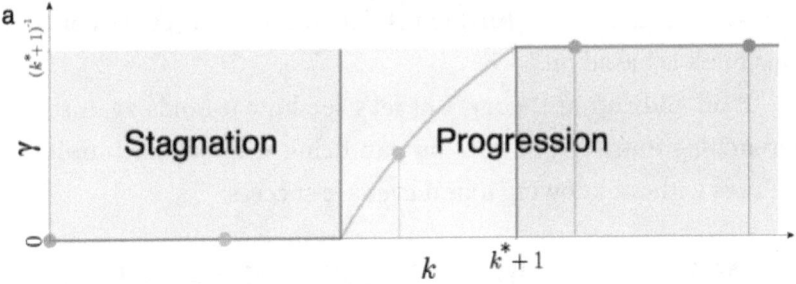

Figure 8—Model for *k* from the Northwestern paper

Those stuck in the stagnation region will never succeed, and those who can break out of stagnation are likely to succeed. Like Jason's point that failure and success live very close to each other, it might only take a small incremental improvement to bust out of the stagnation region.

In an article about the paper, lead researcher Dashun Wang compared how k works to the melting point of ice.[84] When the ambient temperature goes from thirty-one degrees to thirty-two degrees, nothing happens—there's no outward indication of progress. As soon as the temperature hits thirty-three degrees, there's an observable outcome—the ice starts to melt. People in the stagnation region can incrementally improve while continuing to fail without seeing outward signs of progress. They only find success once they hit that inflection point of improvement.

I don't think it's coincidental that the graphic representation of k from the Northwestern paper matches the S-shaped learning curve. The k is a measure of how much learning an individual or group incorporates from a previous attempt into the next—it's a measure of learning. The stagnation region is what we've been calling the Bumpy Part. Their definition of inflection point that leads to success is the same as the one we described in the introduction. Essentially, the Northwestern researchers used their datasets and analysis to further validate the learning curve concept this book is based on.

It all adds up in theory. But let's see how it holds against the wrenching journey of a real human being who suffered multiple failures without knowing if he'd ever see success.

FROM GOLDEN CHILD TO FAILURE AND BACK AGAIN

Jason Christie, one of the most respected and well-published medical researchers in pulmonary and critical care, was a single data point in the NIH grant application database the Northwestern researchers studied. Unlike the other people profiled in this book, Dr. Christie (as I'll call him to distinguish from Jason Lee) was the kid who skipped a grade in elementary school, attended an Ivy League college (Brown), got into another Ivy League school for his medical degree (Columbia), and started his research career at a third Ivy (Penn). Early in his career, his colleagues called him the "golden child" because he showed signs of success in the medical research field at such a young age. It would not be accurate to put Dr. Christie in the category of a "regular" person like you and me. He is clearly a top 1 percent performer in life. Underneath this golden veneer, Dr. Christie faced adversity like the rest of us.

Before becoming a doctor, Dr. Christie was a good high school lacrosse player. However, his success didn't come through raw athletic ability. As he described himself, he had "modest speed, modest strength, and coordination," but through effort, work ethic, and being a true student of the game, he became good enough to play in college until he started having a combination of three concerning health problems in his junior year. First, he developed something called "foot drop," where he was having difficulty lifting the front part of his right foot as he walked. Foot drop isn't a disease; it's a sign of some underlying neurological, muscular, or anatomical problem. Second, he was having serious headaches, especially when the weather would change. The third was even more concerning. Whenever he looked down, he had double vision. The combination of symptoms forced him to stop playing lacrosse, but he managed to stay in school and tried to ignore all three issues.

Doctors thought the headaches and double vision might have been a withdrawal reaction to stopping prednisone, which he had taken for another ailment, and suggested it would go away with time. So, he continued going to school as usual and even sat for his MCATs while this problem was still undiagnosed. To get through the six-hour test with double vision, insanely, he covered his right eye as he looked down to read each question and fill in the correct circle with his No. 2 pencil. Decades later, he said, it "sounds a little bit ridiculous as I say it out loud, but it's what I had to do to get through the test."

Not long after the MCAT, he saw a neurologist who immediately ordered a brain CT scan. The next day, an administrator called and said the CT scan showed something "concerning" and that he needed to come in for another appointment. When he probed for details, the administrator couldn't say. So, for the next six days, he researched what it could be—possibly multiple sclerosis or some other neurodegenerative disease or perhaps a cancerous brain tumor. After six agonizing days, his neurologist hung the CT scan over a lightbox to show an orange-sized meningioma taking up a huge area of Dr. Christie's head. A meningioma is a slow-growth tumor that forms out of the meninges, one of the protective layers around the brain. Ninety-two percent of them are benign, as was this one. It may have been growing for ten or fifteen years and was so large that it was putting pressure on nerves connected to his vision and foot. After agonizing over worst-case scenarios for six days, the diagnosis of a giant brain tumor was ironically a relief. He didn't have cancer or multiple sclerosis, and the tumor could be removed with relatively low-risk surgery. He had to skip finals and get permission to take them the following January, but all in all, this health scare turned out just fine. He went on to finish the academic year on time and did well enough on his one-eyed MCAT to get into Columbia Medical School. Dr. Christie's reaction foreshadowed his matter-of-fact resilience when faced with rejection after rejection of his applications for an NIH R01 grant.

After graduating from medical school, Dr. Christie went into internal medicine and completed his residency and a pulmonary and critical care fellowship at Penn Medical School. Through his residency and critical care fellowship, Dr. Christie realized that many of the decisions doctors made were based on anecdotes and basic physiology rather than data-driven best practices. He wanted to fill those gaps in knowledge with scientifically verified data to help clinicians make better decisions, so he decided to go down the academic research path. His initial interest was in how people recover from lung transplants.

Given Dr. Christie's fellowship came only a decade after the first successful lung transplant in the US, there were many unknowns about how to treat complications of the surgery, especially in dealing with rejection of the donor lung and the injury to the lung caused by the transplant itself. Back in the 1990s, Dr. Christie studied a disease called ARDS (acute respiratory distress syndrome), which became well-known recently because it is an end-stage complication of COVID-19. In addition to COVID-19, ARDS can be caused by pneumonia, sepsis, or lung trauma, including the trauma of a lung transplant. Dr. Christie wanted to understand why some transplant patients suffered from ARDS while others didn't and what possible medical interventions could be taken to prevent it. His research journey started with an NIH career development award, a smaller grant designed to help less experienced investigators gain experience before transitioning to independent research (such as an R01). Dr. Christie was only six months into his research fellowship at Penn when he successfully applied for a career development award to study lung injury—how he first earned the moniker "golden child."

As his career development award money was starting to run out, Dr. Christie's mentors and leadership felt he was ready to be the primary investigator for an independent grant or R01. Of course, the R01 grant awards are much more competitive, but his mentors were confident he would come through like he had on everything else he tried.

Dr. Christie wanted to understand how genetics interplayed with ARDS. That is, could genetic factors contribute to who gets ARDS after lung transplantation or lung trauma? He worked hard on the grant application, describing the importance of this study, how he would execute it, and what he was expecting to learn. Months later, he received a disappointing denial from the reviewers. While the application was good enough to warrant a percentile score (the reviewers thought it could be improved enough to eventually be granted), it was far from approval. The reviewers' comments surprised Dr. Christie, as they seemed unwilling to accept that epidemiologic* approaches to genetics research were valid. Given

---

* Epidemiology is the study of how diseases spread and impact public health. Epidemiologists study the patterns and causes of disease and injury in human populations. Their view is broad versus the family pedigree approach, which studies diseases passed down through specific family trees.

Dr. Christie had gotten a master's degree in epidemiology on the side, he was quite perplexed.

Some of the reviewers completely rejected the possibility of determining a genetic connection to ARDS without a "family pedigree" study. However, ARDS is caused by relatively rare events such as severe trauma, sepsis, or a transplant. So the family pedigree approach would require finding generations of families who happened to suffer these unfortunate events, a pretty infeasible proposition, especially considering ARDS was so recently defined. To Dr. Christie, the best way to understand the genetic influence on ARDS is to follow a large cohort of people who have banked genetic information and see who develops the disease over time—an epidemiological approach. This same cohort methodology helped uncover the genetic factors that protect some people from HIV/AIDS.[85] However, some of the review panel members assigned to Dr. Christie's application had firm beliefs that family pedigree studies were the only way to study genetic diseases.

While disappointed, Dr. Christie's mentors and colleagues weren't worried. NIH R01 award rates hover around 20 percent for any given application,[86] so it's pretty standard not to get a positive response on the first attempt. At the time, applicants could resubmit the same application, with modifications that addressed the reviewer's critiques, two more times before it would have to be abandoned.* Dr. Christie took in all the feedback, consulted with his colleagues, and tried again pretty quickly. Grant applications are only reviewed three times a year, so by the time applicants get their feedback, there's only a month or so left to resubmit on the next cycle. This timing likely plays into the temporal factor in the Northwestern research. If an applicant misses a cycle, they must wait several extra months before being able to resubmit—according to their model, missing a cycle would be indicative of ultimate failure.

Dr. Christie had a lot of learning to apply to his next attempt.

---

* In 2017, the NIH reduced the number of resubmissions to 1.

He simplified the language dramatically and tried to explain why his cohort genetics approach made sense by using concrete examples like the HIV/AIDS case. After sweating out more than a few long nights, he was able to submit his application before the window closed.

Several months later, Dr. Christie was denied a second time. While his percentile score improved, and by the comments, he could tell he won over most of the reviewers, there seemed to be a few stubborn panelists who still wanted him to use a family pedigree approach to the study. Undeterred, Dr. Christie did his best to answer the critiques of the stubborn reviewers and simplify his language even more. He submitted his third and final attempt within the window of the next grant cycle. The results of his third attempt showed an improvement in his percentile score, and according to the commentary, the vast majority of the reviewers felt that this was a valid and scientifically rigorous approach. Yet a small minority of the reviewers contended that Dr. Christie's approach was flawed. With those negative contributions to the score, Dr. Christie missed the approval by two points and had to abandon this application altogether. He was despondent. The golden child had failed three times in a row.

SUPPORTIVE ENVIRONMENTS ENABLE RESILIENCE

Ivy League-educated doctors get rich, right? That's much more likely for practicing clinicians. On the medical research side, people get paid through research grants, from which a portion is used to pay out salaries. Dr. Christie was deeply in debt from all his schooling—in fact, one of the reasons he pursued his master's in epidemiology was to maintain student status to defer his loans until after receiving one of these grants. So Dr. Christie was low on cash, high on debt, and starting a young family. Medical researchers in this position only have so many options. They can declare themselves a failed researcher and try to find a job in the clinical world, or they can leave medicine altogether and try to find employment in another field.

Dr. Christie had a third option that his university provided: an environment of support at Penn that would "bridge" him during this time. Bridging could take the form of paying his salary with university endowment funds or finding other grants to support him. We talked about cultivating a support system in the "Get Help" chapter, but we didn't emphasize finding a supportive institution (whether a university, company, or other large organization). By having the privilege and luck to be part of the hugely supportive environment at Penn, Dr. Christie had perhaps more opportunity to fail before he succeeded than those in less supportive environments. For a while, Penn bridged another researcher who couldn't get funding for an out-of-favor research area that experts of the day said would never work. Her grant applications were rejected so many times that she fell off the full professorship track. This researcher, Katalin Karikó, bridged by her colleagues at Penn for nearly a decade, continued to build her case around mRNA gene therapy. While Penn eventually lost patience with her, those years of bridging were foundational to her work that led to her 2023 Nobel Prize in Physiology and Medicine for contributions to the development of mRNA technology.

• • •

After Dr. Christie's grant proposal was rejected a third time, and he was in a quandary about his career direction, a more senior Penn researcher included Dr. Christie's genetics project in a large NIH program grant, which focused on the molecular mechanisms of ARDS. So, in the end, Dr. Christie was able to complete the genetics research from an epidemiologic perspective under the umbrella of another NIH award. While working on his genetics-based research on ARDS, Dr. Christie started another ambitious project—to establish a standard definition of a syndrome called primary graft dysfunction, a severe and often deadly lung injury that occurs within the first seventy-two hours after a lung transplant.[87] His goal was to get consensus on the definition of the disease and create a multicenter consortium for researchers around the country to study it. Once he established this consortium, Dr. Christie planned to use the data gathered across these disparate research centers to better understand risk factors and mechanisms involved in primary graft dysfunction. This coordinated effort required some funding, so Dr. Christie decided to take another swing at an R01 grant to execute this data collection and analysis exercise.

The former golden child—now a grizzled veteran of grant applications—thought he was going down a much more fruitful path with this line of research. This R01 application proposed using the newly created Lung Transplant Outcomes Group to define clinical, biological, and genetic risk factors for primary graft dysfunction. Yet, months after sending in a much more polished application than his initial line of study, the NIH grant reviewers rejected Dr. Christie again! He couldn't believe it. He had worked so hard to use simple language and added a plethora of concrete examples that assumed the reviewers were less familiar with the details of lung injuries. However, the genetics component returned to haunt him—the reviewers struggled with his epidemiological approach. Dr. Christie was at the end of the bridge, paying his salary and "starting to panic a bit." So, on the next resubmission, he took a different tack. He completely removed the genetics component of the application and resubmitted this "safer" application pretty quickly (attempt number five, if you're counting), and separately, he created another new grant application (number six) that focused only on the genetics component—in Dr. Christie's mind, the riskier approach.

Remember, the variable k from the earlier Northwestern research essentially means how many of the previous failed attempts are incorporated into the next one—the more, the better. Dr. Christie essentially created a two-for-one, incorporating the vast majority of one larger proposal into two different applications. Soon, the response for this safe, genetics-free application came back—rejected *again*. The reviewers wanted more epidemiologic detail and supporting data to approve the grant even without the genetics component. Disappointed but not disheartened, Dr. Christie quickly pulled together and submitted application number seven as a third and final try for this grant.

Meanwhile, the results from his riskier genetics-only application came back. Because this was a new grant application, a different panel reviewed it, and they more fully understood and appreciated Dr. Christie's epidemiological approach, yet this one was still rejected. On his third and final revision of this application—his eighth attempt overall at an NIH R01 award—the panel approved it. "I literally fell off my chair and sat down on the ground. I had finally made it." A few months later, his second revision of the "safer" application was also approved. Dr. Christie went from barely getting by as a researcher bridged by his supportive environment to an independent investigator of two simultaneous NIH R01 grants. This whole process, from the first application to the flurry of submissions at the end, took three years of rejection, learning, and resilience.

The takeaways from Dr. Christie's story and the Northwestern paper predicting success and failure are both simple and profound. When repeatedly trying to succeed at something and running into failure, you should do the following:

1. Carefully consider all feedback and data from your failure.

2. Salvage the "good" aspects of your attempt for your subsequent one.

3. Continue to improve the speed of each attempt and watch for measurable improvements on each iteration.

If you don't see consistent measurable improvement on subsequent attempts, or your timing between attempts does not get shorter, either you're not incorporating enough of the feedback from previous attempts, or perhaps this gig just isn't for you.

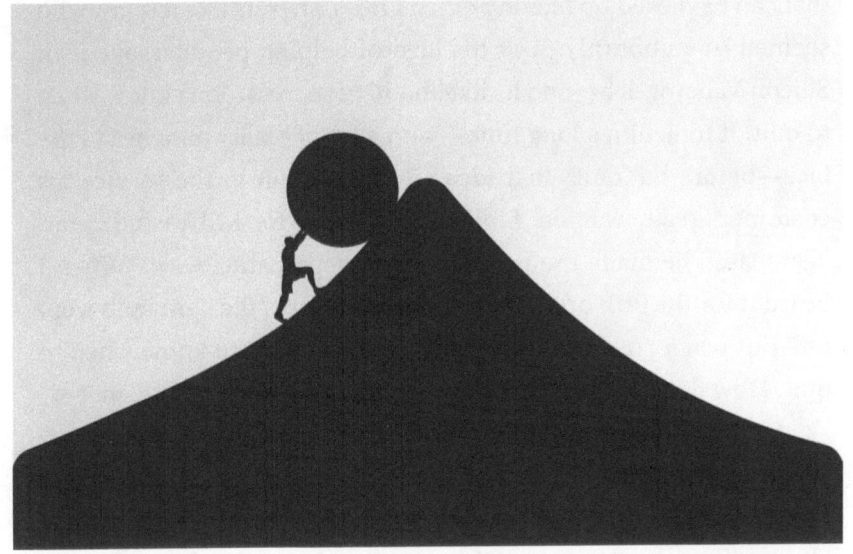

Figure 9—Sisyphus Revisited

HOW TO KNOW WHEN TO QUIT

Consider the "Sisyphus Revisited" graphic above as a metaphor for adversity. Unlike other Sisyphus depictions, this one can actually get to the top of the hill and let the boulder roll down the other side—the equivalent of "making it." On the arduous way up, Sisyphus cannot see the top of the hill—the boulder is in the way (a metaphor for the daily grind). He has no idea how long he will have to keep pushing until he finally reaches the top. Will it be on the next step or perhaps never?

When faced with these uncertainties, how do you know when it's time to quit and let the boulder roll back to where you started, or if you're so close you should keep pushing? This is a valid question whether your adversity is about getting an NIH grant, trying to learn a new complex skill, or working through a personal relationship. After a long, rough go of it, at some point, you have to ask, "Is it time to quit?" The good news is that knowing when to quit is a skill that can be picked up like any other. Often, strivers like Jeremy, who seemed to stubbornly push his idea of helping people make it in Silicon Valley well beyond its likelihood of success, don't know when to quit. It took him a long time—with a lot of reality punches to the face—before he "quit" that idea and moved on to the service his customers really wanted: LinkedIn expertise for MBA candidates. Years later, he made the point in a self-deprecating way: "When I heard it for the fifth or tenth or hundredth time, the light bulb went off." But when you're in the middle of it, it's hard to know when to quit. How do you know that this next attempt won't be the one?

In her thought-provoking book *Quit: The Power of Knowing When to Walk Away*,[88] former world champion poker player and now executive coach and speaker Annie Duke provides compelling observations about quitting. First, she dispels the idea that quitting is a bad thing. If you've read the first 95 percent of this book, you might assume that I think quitting equals failing and that I recommend only resilience and grit. I don't, and—as we saw in the Jeremy case—context matters. Quitting an idea, a job, or even a partner can be the absolute healthiest choice in the right circumstances, and it can even *enable* the success you've been destined for.

When to quit is the hardest decision to make, especially if you've invested a long time in whatever you're trying to accomplish. Humans are well known to fall prey to the sunk cost fallacy: to follow the irrational behavior of continuing an activity simply because they have already spent time and resources on it, even when investing further brings little to no additional value. The logically minded look objectively at the costs and benefits going forward, not considering the previous investment because, of course, you can't change that.

Somehow, our paleolithic brains aren't great at that piece of logic.

Similarly, the problem solvers struggle with "one more thing." They see their failure as a puzzle and want to keep trying one more thing to see if they can fix it. For example, Jeremy was certain that his techniques for making it in Silicon Valley would work for others because it worked for him. Initially, he thought the reasons for his company's continued failure centered on the positioning or marketing, so he continued to iterate them. As a product guy, I often suffered a similar fate, continuously adding just one more feature to a product in hopes that it would transform a failed product into a successful one. In retrospect, most of the time, the additional feature only made the product worse because it muddied the primary purpose of the product or simply made it harder to use. But when you sense the promise that this new feature will be the difference maker—or (in a different quitting context) the hope that your boss won't be a jerk after this last confidence-killing episode or the prospect that your underperforming employee will turn things around—it's really hard to make the quit decision. That's why Duke recommends deciding when to quit *in advance*.

The reality is that most times, you don't know for sure if the "one more thing" won't be a tipping point that swings your activity from failure to success. But when you're in a more rational state of mind, it may be easier to look at your future self and decide, "If I can't figure this out by the end of the year, then I'll move on to something else." Duke calls this "quit criteria," which you commit to, that is, promise yourself, for some future date or attempt. The Northwestern research on failure and success suggests two clear quit criteria: 1) seeing measurable improvement between attempts and 2) decreasing time between attempts. If you don't see those trends, you'll be doomed to the stagnation region. If those criteria aren't being met by your predetermined date, it's time to move on.

To give yourself more accountability, ask someone to be your "quitting coach" who will hold you to your promise to quit. A quitting coach is a person you respect and trust to be honest with you even if they know their recommendations might hurt. It's best to choose a quitting coach who will be objective and able to balance emotional intelligence with analytical skills. Without a quitting coach, people tend to cheat themselves and keep going for longer or come up with a new "one more thing." If there really is a great "one more thing," consult your quitting coach, and maybe they'll agree, but you should set another quit criterion in case that one doesn't work out either.

NARROW FAILURES CAN LEAD TO GREATER SUCCESS

The Northwestern researchers found another startling revelation from the NIH grant application data for which Dr. Christie served as a data point. In a separate paper published in *Nature*, "Early Career Setback and Future Career Impact,"[89] the researchers separated first-time NIH R01 grant applicants into two cohorts: "narrow win" applicants, whose scores were barely above the threshold to receive a grant, and "near miss" applicants, who were close to receiving a grant but just missed.* The researchers were able to define the two groups in such a way that the scores of the "near miss" and "narrow win" applicants were so close that they were statistically the same. As we can tell from Dr. Christie's story, a fair amount of randomness contributes to the scores depending on who is assigned to review any particular grant and their biases about the research topic. So, members of the "near miss" and "narrow win" groups are essentially randomly assigned.

After separating the first-time applicants into these two groups, the Northwestern researchers studied the careers of the two cohorts. In the "near miss" group, 12 percent left medical research altogether and went on to become clinicians or changed careers completely. Sadly, they disappeared from the medical research

---

* The Northwestern researchers normalized and anonymized the data in such a way that we can't tell if Dr. Christie's first attempt fit into the "near miss" category. However, as you'll see, Dr. Christie's successful career indicated that he performed like he was part of that group.

world, never to contribute again. This finding is even sadder when considering the "near miss" applicants who went on to make another grant application *systematically outperformed* those in the "narrow win" cohort.

Those who failed to get their first NIH application granted

- Published 12 percent more papers.

- Had 21 percent more "hit papers" (those in the top 5 percent of citations).

- Published 50 percent more papers that included a clinical trial, an indication that the paper had potential for real impact.

So, applicants who were knocked down, like Dr. Christie, got back up and systematically outperformed those who were never knocked down. To be clear, this performance advantage for the "near miss" group was maintained, even accounting for the attrition rate of those who never applied for a grant again, among other confounding factors. The next logical question is "Why?"

The researchers examined what they called the screening hypothesis—that early failures screened out less determined people, leaving only those more likely to succeed in the pool. However, their calculations indicate that screening did not account for all the difference between the two groups. The researchers hypothesized two more reasons an early setback helped people in their careers.

- **Failure teaches valuable lessons** that are simply harder to learn otherwise. That's my personal experience. Life lessons are real.

- **Success breeds complacency**. People who succeed on their first try just don't work as hard or as intensely as those who've suffered a setback.

ARE THE WINNERS ACTUALLY LOSERS?

Hypothesis #2 suggests that the "narrow win" researchers may have ultimately had less productive careers *because* they succeeded on their first attempt. I've encountered a few anecdotal stories that support this finding.

For example, entrepreneurs who create a huge hit on their first business but never repeat their success again. There are many serial entrepreneurs, but few produce winner after winner. In a similar vein, I've come across salespeople who had a giant win early in their career, but after that big sale, they have trouble replicating more big sales wins.

Whether you've had early wins or early failures, what matters most is how you respond to those experiences. If you've been winning your whole life, think about the possibility that you could be even more successful with a bit more grit and intensity. And if a setback hits you, take your lumps like everyone profiled in this book and recognize it as an opportunity to learn. It might be just what you need to reach greater heights. Another name for taking lumps in exchange for improvement is "antifragile."

WHAT'S THE OPPOSITE OF FRAGILE?

Think of an elegant, exquisitely thin wine glass with a large, shapely bowl. Now consider an errant elbow knocking the top-heavy glass onto a quartz countertop. It doesn't take much to turn this beautiful glass into shards. Thicker glass might make it less fragile, but it would still break if it fell from a high shelf. Do some objects or systems behave in the opposite way—actually *benefiting* from the shock of an impact? In his brilliant book *Antifragile: Things That Gain from Disorder*, Nassim Nicholas Taleb profoundly observes that a wide variety of naturally occurring and complex human-created systems actually get better from some level of volatility, stress, or disorder. Further, the reciprocal is often true: many antifragile systems get weaker if they are not stressed.

An obvious example of an antifragile system is your own muscular system. The process of strength training (the stressor) creates microtears in your muscles. Your body recognizes the minor injury and grows the muscle back bigger and stronger than before the stress of weight training. Without some level of stress, your muscles atrophy—they need the stressors to flourish. Of course, even antifragile systems have a limit to the stress they can endure. For example, stressing a bicep too much may result in a tear or other injury. However, within limits, stressing the muscle only has benefits.

Once your eyes are open to this concept, you see antifragile systems everywhere. For example, a fascinating 2020 *Scientific American* article describes "Why We Have So Many Problems with Our Teeth."[90] The observation is that these days, nine out of ten people have teeth that are at least slightly misaligned, and three-quarters of us have wisdom teeth that do not fit in our mouths. Yet, when we look at the fossil record of our ancestor's teeth, theirs are most often beautifully aligned, along with perfectly functional wisdom teeth. Why is that? Our modern food choices don't put enough stress on our teeth that evolved to chew on much tougher material. By making food "easier," we seemingly wrecked our teeth. That is, by reducing stress, antifragile systems start to break down.

In addition to natural systems, many human inventions display antifragile properties. While volatility makes these systems better, our culture tends to reduce volatility, which often feels better in the short run but weakens the system over time. Think about aggressively customized news feeds that allow people to stay comfortably in their belief bubble versus struggling with opposing opinions. Antibiotic overuse may make individuals more comfortable in the short term, but it enables hyper-resistant superbugs to take over. Or Taleb's favorite: bank bailouts reduce short-term stress on the economy but lower banker accountability and encourage reckless risk-taking in the future.

Taleb argues that pretty much all markets are antifragile. He apparently made an enormous amount of money creating his own financial instrument that essentially bet on *steep* market volatility (versus betting on up or down). No one can predict when markets will go up or down, but eventually, markets will be volatile (that is, go up or down by a lot). If you're an individual player in a market, whether it's a stock market, the real estate market, or the dating market, preparing yourself for volatility gives you the best chance for success when an inevitable shock happens. One market relevant to this book is the employment market.

As mentioned, career advice and our educational system lean toward picking a single field early in life and aggressively specializing—acquiring niche skills tailored to a specific role within that niche. Specializing may feel comfortable because you can build competence in the field and not have to work too hard thereafter. It also feels like it provides security. However, specialization actually increases fragility in careers by reducing optionality. Optionality, giving yourself a bunch of ways out of a surprisingly negative or volatile situation, is a great way to protect yourself against fragility. Getting locked into a specialized career path makes it much harder to change fields if that area declines, gets boring, or "life happens." In contrast, developing a broad base of versatile skills makes your career more antifragile by creating lifelong career optionality. So go ahead and get a data science degree—that's hot right now. But make sure you have serious outside interests in film, political science, auto mechanics, or some other orthogonal skill. This way, you'll be much more likely to handle volatility like a layoff, AI taking over data science jobs, or some other unpredictable event (a "black swan," as Taleb calls it). A person with a variety of skills and interests preserves the options of data scientist, policy analyst, film critic, or auto mechanic. Accepting career uncertainty in the short term unlocks greater potential and antifragility in the long run—another vote for the jack-of-all-trades career path.

• • •

While he doesn't explicitly use the word antifragile, Stanford professor of neurobiology and ophthalmology and popular podcaster Andrew Huberman describes the process of learning and neuroplasticity as an antifragile system.[91] Neuroplasticity refers to the brain's remarkable capacity to rewire and restructure itself when we take in new information or have new experiences. The rewiring of the brain is the biological activity that underlies learning. Fascinatingly, what Huberman reported, based on Eric Knudsen's experiments on owl brains,[92] is that neuroplasticity or learning *only* seems to happen when there are errors or mismatches in what the brain predicts and what actually happens. "The way to create plasticity is to send signals to the brain that something is wrong, something is different, and something isn't being achieved." Put another way, the brain is an antifragile system that requires errors or mismatches to improve and—without the stress of error conditions—will atrophy just like your muscles.

The Northwestern article describing "near miss" NIH grant applicants who went on to have better careers than the "narrow win" researchers, the ideas behind Taleb's antifragile systems that thrive on shock and volatility, and Huberman's point that errors are required for learning all point to the same conclusion: failure is required to learn, and early failure leads to future success.

When you fail at something, know it's simply a step toward getting better.

LIGHTEN UP

Okay, but failing sucks. It feels like crap. It hurts. It's exhausting. It's humbling. Most of all, it's discouraging. How can people face the adversity of failing to maintain resilience for the next attempt? Helen, the artist rejected from art school, took a break and then slowly got back into making art for the joy of it. "After a few months of licking my wounds, I thought, I love the possibility that art brings. I'm just gonna carry on making it." Dr. Christie continued after multiple rejections, largely because his supportive environment assured him that he was doing good work and convinced him he'd be successful one day. Another way to face failure attempts is to reframe the situation as we did at the end of the last section: "know it's simply a step toward getting better." Back in the "Get Help" chapter, when we converted the "rejection rate" of your network reach into "conversion rate," that was an example of reframing the situation. The numbers are the same, but because of the way our brains work, it sure makes us feel better.

• • •

Chase's method to reframe the situation was to inject humor into everything he did, even though he was in one of the most unfunny situations anyone could imagine, finding himself a quadriplegic. Humor was a tool he had in his bag from being the high school class clown and part of the stand-up comedy world. (Chase's job before the accident was project manager for nationally renowned stand-ups such as Bert Kriescher and Taylor Tomlinson.)

For most of his first month, not only was Chase completely paralyzed from the shoulders down, but he had also contracted COVID at that supposedly safe Philadelphia New Year's party. So, everyone had to stay away from him for weeks. In dire need of human contact and entertainment, Chase set up a local Philadelphia Tinder account with no intention of meeting anyone. He just wanted to talk to people and cheer himself up. His profile included actual pictures of him in his hospital bed with a massive neck brace holding his head in place and his face still bruised and swollen from his fall. The playfully inappropriate bio read, "Recently paralyzed. My neck brace holds up to 150 pounds. Come take a seat." Chase's leaning into his dark humor didn't stop there. He swiped left and right using voice commands (later, he even used swiping as a rehab exercise to improve his hand and arm motor skills). When he got a match, things got interesting. People would say nice things like, "You have beautiful eyes," and Chase would come back with "Thanks! That's the only working part of my body."

Later, Chase matched with a nursing student who said, "What the fuck did you do to your neck?" He responded, "I saw you were a nursing student, so I hurt myself. But fuck. I think I'm at the wrong hospital." She responded, "LMFAO, there's no way you just said that to me." Chase followed with "Where you at, girl? Imma request a transfer ASAP."

Chase used humor in just about every aspect of his recovery, from spending his non-rehab time binging *The Office* to making dark, self-deprecating jokes around the nursing and rehab staff to even his goal-setting, as you'll see soon. Reframing his dreadful situation with dark, stark, and self-aware humor made Chase more resilient during the most grueling days of recovery.

SMILE AT YOUR STRESS

Reframing a difficult situation with humor worked for Chase, but what if being funny is not your bag? Is it possible to reframe stressful situations in other ways to become more resilient when you're hitting a rough patch? Conventional wisdom on how emotional stress affects human health is clearly negative. It's easy to find internet articles describing how stress causes everything from the common cold to heart disease. Health psychologist Kelly McGonigal suggests just the opposite—that stress is good for you, but there's a twist. In *The Upside of Stress: Why Stress Is Good for You, and How to Get Good at It*,[93] McGonigal references a University of Wisconsin–Madison study[94] that examined the relationship between the amount of stress people experience and their *perception* of whether stress affects their health.

The researchers compared the 1998 National Health Interview Survey with over 28,000 subjects and public mortality records through 2006. A key question in the initial health survey was "Do you believe that stress is harmful to your health?" The shocking finding was that those who both reported having high stress and *thought* that stress was harmful to their health were 43 percent more likely to die by 2006 than those who also reported high stress but didn't think stress was harmful to their health!

This finding suggests that it's not the stress that's harmful; it's the worrying about the stress that causes the damage. McGonigal goes on to propose that by reframing your perception of stress, you can turn it into an asset versus a liability. That is, when you recognize your body is reacting to a stressful situation with a racing heartbeat, quickened breath, or sweat on your upper lip, instead of reinforcing the feelings of stress, you should recognize the truth about your body—you're having a fight-or-flight response. The fight-or-flight response evolved over millions of years through many species before ours to empower you, protect you, and make you stronger when you need to be stronger. You breathe harder to enrich your blood with more oxygen. Your heart races to pump more oxygen-rich blood into your brain to sharpen it and prepare your muscles for quick, decisive movement. In small doses, your bodily stress reaction is *helpful*. If you think about it that way, you're more likely to use your stress to empower yourself while the stressful moment is at hand and calm yourself down when the stressful situation is over.

I suspect the people in the Wisconsin study who felt that stress was harmful would start with a stressful situation and "death spiral" (literally) by freaking out about how stressed they were, which caused them to become more stressed and prolong this fight-or-flight response well beyond its useful value. Long-term, constant stress is not healthy (supporting all those internet articles). Controlled, empowering stress prepares you for a fight or flight and helps you decide when the danger is over and to calm down. Use your stress as a powerful tool for resiliency when you hit the Bumpy Parts of the learning curve.

GOALS THAT ENGAGE OTHERS

If you've read any book like this, you've probably been waiting for the "goal-setting" section. Of course, setting goals is incredibly important for accountability, measuring progress, and marking a moment in time for gratitude and celebration. That said, setting goals is also advice a well-meaning high school counselor might offer. One answer to the question of *how* you set effective goals is to construct them in such a way that they are not only ambitious but also rally your entire support system around you. When Chase's doctors told him to set goals, he had fun with it and designed his goals to bring joy and laughter to his family, friends, and broader social network. Chase's choice of goals engaged and grew his support system, rallied support, and forced higher accountability.

Since finger dexterity was a critical first step to his recovery and ability to live independently, Chase made his first goal to give "the finger." He tells the story in a hilarious TikTok that's pinned to the top of his page (@chasegetsbetter). The TikTok starts with some cool jazz and Chase jiggling his shoulders to the music (it's all the dancing his body could muster at the time). Then it says, "55 days ago I was paralyzed completely from the shoulders down . . . And after all this time my left hand is finally doing the only thing it needs to do." In time with the music, the video abruptly cuts to Chase giving the finger to the camera, then to his physical therapists, and even to a sad-looking service dog. It's all celebratory and fun-loving, and not at all obvious how much grueling practice and effort it took Chase to teach his body to hold up his arm and arrange his fingers in the famous "bird" pose. Chase didn't dwell on the hard parts—he focused on the joy of reaching his goal and sharing it.

The physical therapists suggested Chase should have a second goal around walking. Some people might make the goal to walk up and down the hall of the rehab hospital. That wasn't bold enough for Chase. Since he was in Philadelphia, why not walk up the famous "Rocky Steps"? When he told the doctors about his plan, they said, "Be more realistic. . . . Don't go there yet. Make it more grounded."

The doctors weren't being overly cautious. At this point, Chase had no motor function—it was only a couple of days after the accident. Yet, Chase responded to the doctors who wanted him to set a more realistic walking goal: "No, no, no! I'm crazy. I'm gonna do the crazy thing." Within a couple of months of setting the goal, Chase started walking with the help of a "vector," a giant harness that holds most of the patient's weight while they stimulate their walking muscles on a treadmill. "I would do everything in my power to pull my leg through. In the beginning, I would take like five steps and then be more tired than I've ever been in my entire life." After weeks of grueling work, Chase was getting close, so he invited his friends and family to come to Philadelphia to witness his Rocky Steps climb. He even made a hype TikTok telling people the date and time of his attempt.

Only seventy-nine days after his injury, Chase rolled up to the Rocky Steps in a wheelchair. A small crowd was already there, and it grew as tourists gathered to see what the commotion was all about. Chase fed off the energy of the people cheering him on as he stepped out of his wheelchair and transitioned to a walker to get a little closer. Nearby street performers stopped their show and switched their music to "Gonna Fly Now (Theme From *Rocky*)" just as Chase dramatically abandoned his walker and started his awkward but determined climb. With only a physical therapist trailing him, Chase made it up the seventy-two steps in just six minutes and triumphantly raised his arms like Rocky at the top. The local NBC affiliate caught it all on video, and Chase made that evening's NBC10 News telecast. An article the following day in the *Philadelphia Inquirer* also documented Chase's injury and amazing feat. With this ambitious goal and showman's approach, Chase rallied the whole city of Philadelphia behind him to achieve his second goal.

Chase's third goal was born out of a chat thread with some buddies back in San Diego. Chase thought it would be hilarious if his goal was kicking someone in the balls. From a physical therapy perspective, it would require him to balance on two feet and execute the kick by balancing on one foot, quite an advanced set of skills at this stage of his recovery. The only problem was that no one wanted to be Chase's victim. Finally, one of his friends volunteered, who, full disclosure, is one of my aforementioned twin sons. Chase's pair of TikTok videos documenting the event is worth watching. The first one tells Chase's story from the accident through his training for the big kick, and the second includes the hilarious and truly painful kick and celebration. As of this writing, the pair of ball-kicking TikToks has over 13.5M combined views. Chase had learned how to harness the power of social media for support, and it had become a significant contributing factor in his personal fight for recovery.

GRATITUDE BOLSTERS RESILIENCE

I used to hate thanking people. As a kid, my mother would nag me to send thank-you notes or, God forbid, call relatives to thank them for a $10 birthday gift. The nine-year-old version of me thought the whole process was cringy and a complete waste of time. I clearly didn't understand gratitude.

Of course, a "thank-you" is meaningless unless true gratitude inspires it.

Even though I feel real gratitude around my wonderful family, my health, and even thoughtful gifts, I never made the connection between gratitude and how it could affect other aspects of my well-being. Writing this book and learning from people like Chase, Helen, and Dr. Christie, who, at their lowest points, found a way to be grateful, has changed my mind. I realized that gratitude is another effective way to reframe a negative situation. As Chase said, "The doctors told me that if I had hit myself half a centimeter in another direction, I'd be dead. Looking at it from that point of view, I'm grateful to be alive. . . . I was like, since I'm here, I might as well enjoy it." Chase's gratitude helped him to recover and made him more resilient, but is there data that allows us to extrapolate this idea more broadly?

• • •

Gratitude has been a part of the human condition since the beginning of time, but a quick look on trends.google.com shows the word has been consistently and continuously searched more frequently over the last twenty years, with spikes every November for Thanksgiving and understandable dips in 2020 and 2021 likely due to COVID.

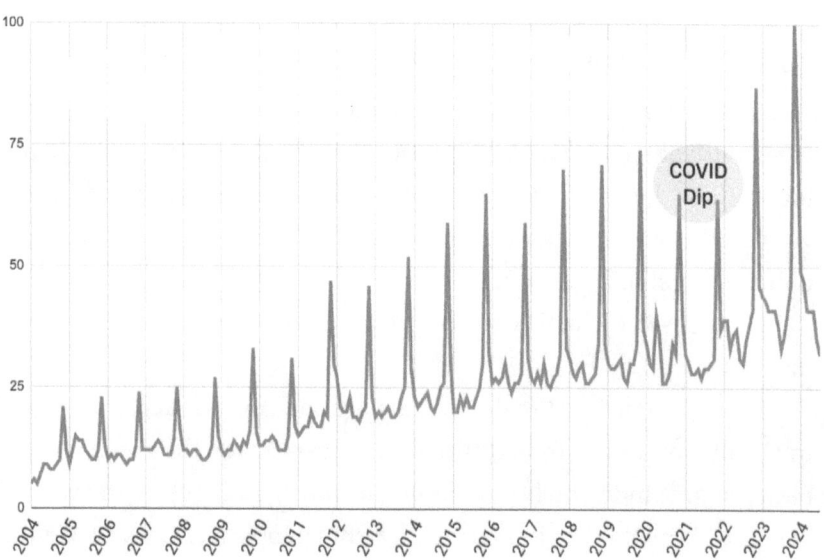

Figure 10—Searches on the word "gratitude" over time.
Source: Google Trends

COVID inadvertently created an amazing natural experiment to understand how gratitude affects peoples' reactions to adversity. Researchers at the University of Nebraska asked over 200 college students to complete a standardized gratitude questionnaire assessing the subjects' "appreciation of positive experiences in daily life." The deadline to submit answers happened to be March 15, 2020.[95] On March 16, COVID-19 restrictions were imposed on campus, so everyone in the study was simultaneously hit with an anxiety-provoking and confusing bump in the road.

The researchers repeated the gratitude questionnaire at the end of April 2020 when the news only continued to get worse, and the future was still quite unclear. The second survey included additional questions about how subjects were feeling about the COVID situation. Surprisingly, the researchers found that those who scored higher on the gratitude scale on the first questionnaire were more resilient in their reaction to COVID-19. That is, they were more likely to report *positive* life changes due to the pandemic, including strengthened relationships, more free time, academic improvements, and better mental health. Conversely, those lower on the gratitude scale had a far more *negative* reaction to the pandemic, including a higher preponderance of depressive symptoms, anxiety, and negative outlooks. It's not clear if gratitude causes or correlates with resilience, but given what we've learned about positivity and self-deception, coupled with stories like Chase's, it seems likely to be causative. Said another way, cultivating gratitude builds resilience.

The researchers discuss several theories about why those higher on the gratitude scale reacted so positively toward the COVID epidemic. The three concepts they describe include

- **The broaden-and-build theory**, which proposes that gratitude, as a positive emotion, may broaden one's thinking and build lasting personal resources that can be drawn upon during difficult times.

- **The undoing hypothesis**, which suggests that gratitude might counteract the effects of negative emotions.

- **The incompatibility theory**, that gratitude may be incompatible with negative states like depression and anxiety, potentially displacing these harmful thought patterns.

These theories indicate that by practicing gratitude, you can build lasting mental resources that can help you navigate future challenges more effectively. Cultivating gratitude builds resilience.

HOW TO CULTIVATE GRATITUDE

Like most healthy practices (e.g., eating right or exercising), you can't just start being grateful "when you need it." The benefits of gratitude build over time. By practicing gratitude daily, being truly thankful for your life situation, you should be in a better position to respond well to the next looming crisis. While I found a range of methods for cultivating gratitude, everything from "gratitude journaling" to a "gratitude jar," here are three that feel pretty natural:

- **Express gratitude while walking around.** I walk pretty much everywhere and am lucky enough to be in beautiful cities or natural surroundings most of the time. I find myself consciously appreciating things like architecture, public art, or natural beauty and often take a moment to be grateful that I experience it.

- **Reflect on challenges.** Sometimes I ruminate on problems or challenges. When I catch myself in negative self-talk, I stop and reflect on what I have learned or could learn from these things. I only figured this one out in the last few years.

- **Sincerely thank people.** I've grown up quite a bit from that selfish nine-year-old and make a practice to authentically and sincerely thank people for everything from small acts of kindness to supportive phone calls to just being there for me.

So, if you're bouncing hard on the Bumpy Part of the learning curve on the way to that inflection point, step back, take a breath, and remember what you have. Practicing gratitude will make you feel better and will likely improve your resiliency for the next bump in the road.

KEEP YOUR EYE ON THE PRIZE

Our last piece of clichéd advice a helpful school counselor might offer is to "keep your eye on the prize." What does that mean, and how might you do that? Isabel used her purpose as a motivator when she fought through all the math and science prerequisites to get into the aerospace engineering program. She didn't care about the math but knew she had to get through it to become an aerospace engineer. Several other subjects used similar tactics. For example, Chase, when asked how he got through the grueling rehab process and occasional setbacks in his recovery, said, "If you're fully dedicated to it, and it matters more than anything else, you can do it. But if you're not willing to sacrifice things or give it the attention it needs, it's not gonna happen." Said that way, it seems pretty simple. For Chase, getting his physical health back did matter more than anything else—it was his intrinsic purpose.

Dr. Christie felt the same way about contributing to the health of people suffering from lung injuries and disease. In one of our conversations, he cited the tenets of Daniel Pink's *Drive: The Surprising Truth About What Motivates Us*[96]—that there are three elements that drive human motivation: autonomy, mastery, and purpose. Dr. Christie made it clear that purpose was high on his personal hierarchy of motivators. While autonomy around his ideas and mastery of his research skills mattered, he stressed that the ability to fulfill his sense of purpose by way of his research was critical for his perseverance. He continued to stubbornly push his lines of investigation forward because he deeply cared about the potential to prevent complications and save more lives. The science itself wasn't just an abstract intellectual exercise—it meaningfully served suffering patients. This higher purpose, aligned to his talents and interests, is what kept Dr. Christie resilient through setbacks where others may have given up or switched paths.

Isabel's, Chase's, and Dr. Christie's stories reinforce that reminding yourself of your purpose is *critical* to maintaining resilience. When you're down in the trenches fighting adversity, that's a perfect time to circle back to your purpose. Keeping your ultimate goal top of mind will motivate you to outsmart the learning curve.

PRACTICAL GUIDE/SUMMARY

- Embrace your failures as the path to success. Look back critically and take feedback honestly, not only on the items you'll fix next time but on what went right. Leveraging the value of the good keeps you from starting from scratch and the stagnation region, from which you may never leave.

- Recognize that success and failure live really close to each other. There are two measures to determine how close you are to success: 1) *are you improving by a measurable amount between attempts?* and 2) *is the time between attempts decreasing?*

- Set "quit criteria" in advance when you've already been through a lot. Engage a "quitting coach" to hold you accountable.

- Look to join or be a part of supportive environments to prop your resilience up like Dr. Christie found with Penn Medical School. The value of a supportive environment may be the difference between success and failure.

- Think about your career and your life in terms of antifragility. How can you protect yourself from inevitable stress, volatility, or disorder? Increased optionality in the form of a wide variety of interests and activities or ways out of a situation can help.

- From a biological perspective, failure is required to learn. Further, early failure can lead to future success. So when you fail at something, know it's simply a step toward getting better.

- When fighting adversity in the Bumpy Part of the learning curve, reframe the situation with humor and gratitude. Know that stress can be an asset. Keep returning back to why you're doing this—your purpose.

For more extensive guidance and exercises to build resilience, check out the *Outsmart the Learning Curve* Workbook at https://www.outsmartbook.com/workbook or use the QR code below.

CONCLUSION

There are no ordinary people.
You have never talked to a mere mortal.
—C.S. Lewis

MARTHA FINALLY SHARES HER STORY

Three months after Martha told her immigration story for the first time to that boy from Salinas, she received an internal email announcing Adobe's Diversity Conference, now an annual company-wide event meant to "celebrate the uniqueness of Adobe's people, product, and purpose." Along with the announcement, the email included a request for keynote speakers who could share their diversity stories with 1,200 attending executives. Martha's first thought was *If they only knew my diversity story. Here I was [working] with people from Harvard, Stanford, and Yale all around me, and I'm coming from a grass shack?* Could she possibly break her vow of silence? While she always wanted to be a public speaker, sharing her story went against everything she'd been taught. Then she thought about the advice she'd given her own two daughters—if they had an opportunity to do something they always wanted, they should do it. In that moment, Martha decided she was going to submit the application.

As we might expect, Martha's story was so mind-blowing to the diversity team, they had to call her to make sure she wasn't exaggerating. As Martha spelled out her immigration and coming-of-age story, it confirmed how valuable it would be to share with the company. So they asked Martha to be the *closing keynote* of the conference.

Martha's speech was transformative. After walking off the stage to a standing ovation, she essentially never stopped talking about her immigrant story. She told her story on podcasts, including one hosted by tech luminary Guy Kawasaki, and later started her own podcast *Moments with Martha*. She also wrote her story in a children's book and continues to this day to distribute the book to elementary schools all over the country, in both English and Spanish. Her mission is to "put this little book of hope in as many hands of children as possible.... I want everyone to know that where we begin is *only* that—the beginning."

WHAT'S YOUR STORY?

When I started telling people the beats of this book—how I found seven regular people who made dramatic transformations or overcame significant obstacles and then looked for threads of wisdom among them—one of the most common questions was "How did you find these people?" Initially, I simply Googled and eventually found a couple of my subjects that way (Helen and Jeremy). But my "conversion rate" on reaching out wasn't great, and after weeks of internet research and several fruitless AI chatbot conversations, I woke up and realized that I should be looking at my own network. My LinkedIn friend Martha posted updates to her amazing life story all the time. In fact, there were half a dozen additional people, within two degrees of separation of my own network, with just as fascinating and instructive stories as the seven I chose. Moreover, when I started telling people stories about my subjects' transformations, it often reminded them of a friend or relative who had some similar amazing story or used one of the many techniques discussed above.

Clearly, lots of people have fascinating backstories of facing adversity, and the ubiquity of these stories confirmed for me that *everyone has a story, is working on one, or could benefit from starting their next one*, including you. You picked up this book because you see potential in yourself to improve your life or work situation, further your success, or perhaps make a dramatic transformation. I hope the people and findings in this book inspire you to find your true glimmer and turn it into a purpose. Or if you're already on your path, I hope you use the insights to improve, find success, or simply live a more fulfilling life. Yes, the learning curve is bumpy, but by staying open, taking advantage of a supportive network, building confidence through determined practice, and using reframing techniques to stay resilient, you can outsmart the learning curve to achieve everything you're looking for.

● ● ●

In the spirit of openness, I encourage you to pay forward the learnings from this book by sharing it with others who could benefit. Tell friends or colleagues who are looking to improve themselves about the techniques for transformation outlined here. Gift the book to someone you think needs inspiration or guidance. And if you know an extraordinary story of adversity and triumph, make sure to spread that story so it can motivate others. By paying forward the messages in this book, you become part of the broader story of progress.

Another powerful way to pay it forward is to leave an honest review on Amazon. Your feedback helps other readers discover these inspiring stories and insights, ensuring that they reach those who need them most. By taking a moment to share your thoughts, no matter how brief, you become an integral part of this book's mission to inspire improvement, transformation, and success. Your review is a small but powerful act of generosity that can make a significant difference in someone else's journey.

Share Your Review

ACKNOWLEDGMENTS

I AM PROFOUNDLY grateful to the seven remarkable people who were courageous enough to share their deeply personal stories of adversity and transformation in this book.

Martha Niño, whose inspiring children's book describing her immigration story can be purchased for individuals or gifted to whole classrooms at marthanino.com.

Isabel Cardoso, who is now pursuing her PhD while continuing her important work at Lockheed Martin.

Helen Wells, who is growing her business teaching art and selling her vibrant pieces. Enjoy her art at helenwellsartist.com.

Jason Lee, who was named one of the Top 20 Enterprising Leaders of 2023 by MSN. Get a sense of his lighthearted social media persona at youtube.com/@Jasonjosephlee.

Jeremy Schifeling, who is providing the latest tools to empower job hunters with his new book *Career Coach GPT*. Discover his latest projects at thejobinsiders.com.

Chase Friedman, who has progressed so far that he was able to complete a 5K and is now thinking about hiking up Mount Kilimanjaro. Continue following his recovery on TikTok: @chasegetsbetter.

Dr. Jason Christie, who went on to be awarded thirty-nine more NIH grants, totaling nearly $40 million, with the resulting research having saved countless lives. Explore his vital work at www.med.upenn.edu/apps/faculty/index.php/g275/p13080.

I'm also incredibly thankful for the many people who supported me, cheered me on, and bravely gave me the cold, hard truth about my work as it progressed. First, my patient, kind wife, Mary Sipher, who has the skill to switch careers and become a copy editor, if she only had a glimmer in that area. Next, a heartfelt thank-you to my daughter, Ali Sipher, who may have been my most valuable critic and confidant through this process. A special thank-you also to my sister, Lynn Sipher, who helped shape the book by applying her compassionate lens on the world to every word she reviewed. And, of course, I can't forget my talented and supportive writing coach, Nicola Wheir, who guided me through every step of the publishing process.

A deep thank-you to all the people who reviewed early drafts, who were gracious enough with their time for interviews, or who collaborated on ideas and suggested potential subjects, including Michelle Azimov, Andrea Butter, Charles Cushing, Sarah Dobson, Lee Epting, Jonah Gutenberg, Bruce Jacobs, Prashant Mahajan, Jeremy Kahn, Lori Mazan, Kathi McShane, Danny Parris, Kate Purmal, Denise Robinson, Bill Rogers, Ari Roisman, Melina Schaefer, Dan Sipher, Devan Sipher, Josh Sipher, Christine Tao, Laura Thompson, Ben Villagra, and Heather Yurovsky.

Last, I want to acknowledge that, yes, I used AI to write this book. If you use these tools with any depth, you know an AI chatbot couldn't come close to writing this book (at least as I write this in 2024). But my AI tool of choice, Anthropic's Claude, served as a valuable research assistant. I couldn't depend on Claude to actually write anything, and it consistently hallucinated nonexistent research links, but using it for tasks it was good at saved me hours.

For example, in a passage about Helen, I wanted to illustrate the Slade School of Art's esteemed reputation. Name-dropping a few famous alumni familiar to readers would be easy, right? Wrong! A quick glance at the Slade School of Art Wikipedia page shows nearly 200 "notable alumni" dating back to the nineteenth century—none of whom looked familiar to me. Before AI, I might have spent hours combing through each artist's work to see if they created something familiar to my readers.

Instead, I pasted the alumni list into an AI chat window and asked it to give me a few names who've created famous pieces that might be well-known to US readers. A few seconds later, the AI returned sculptor Anish Kapoor, who created Chicago's Cloud Gate, and pop artist Peter Blake, famous for his *Sgt. Pepper's Lonely Hearts Club Band* album cover art. I double-checked the output (as you always should), and it was right! Hours of research turned into a few minutes.

AI can be a tool for good.

ENDNOTES

1. Wikipedia Contributors. 2019. "List of U.S. Cities with Large Hispanic Populations." Wikipedia. Wikimedia Foundation. August 29, 2019. https://en.wikipedia.org/wiki/List_of_U.S._cities_with_large_Hispanic_populations.

2. Mullaney, P. J. "Qualitative Ultrasound Training: Defining the Learning Curve." Clinical Radiology 74, no. 4 (April 1, 2019): 327.e7-327.e19. https://doi.org/10.1016/j.crad.2018.12.018.

3. Purfürst, Frank Thomas. "Learning Curves of Harvester Operators," December 20, 2010. https://hrcak.srce.hr/63720.

4. Parry, Bryan R., and Sheila Williams. "COMPETENCY AND THE COLONOSCOPIST a LEARNING CURVE." Australian and New Zealand Journal of Surgery 61, no. 6 (June 1, 1991): 419–22. https://doi.org/10.1111/j.1445-2197.1991.tb00254.x.

5. Iyengar, Sheena S., Rachael E. Wells, and Barry Schwartz. "Doing Better but Feeling Worse." Psychological Science 17, no. 2 (February 1, 2006): 143–50. https://doi.org/10.1111/j.1467-9280.2006.01677.x.

6. Simon, Herbert A. 1955. "A Behavioral Model of Rational Choice." Quarterly Journal of Economics 59 (1): 99-118.

7. Liu, Jennifer. "Almost Half of Older Millennials Wish They'd Chosen

a Different Career Path—what They'd Do Differently." CNBC, June 17, 2021. https://www.cnbc.com/2021/06/17/nearly-half-of-older-millennials-wish-theyd-chosen-a-different-career.html.

8   Duffy, Ryan D., and William E. Sedlacek. "The Presence of and Search for a Calling: Connections to Career Development." Journal of Vocational Behavior 70, no. 3 (June 1, 2007): 590–601. https://doi.org/10.1016/j.jvb.2007.03.007.

9   Flash was a popular technology that could be used for interactive web pages, animations, and games. It was known to be a somewhat finicky development environment on which it was difficult to create stable, performant applications. Steve Jobs famously banned Flash on iOS, which was the beginning of the end for the technology.

10 Weiss-Sidi, Merav, and Hila Riemer. "Help Others—be Happy? The Effect of Altruistic Behavior on Happiness Across Cultures." *Frontiers in Psychology* 14 (June 23, 2023). https://doi.org/10.3389/fpsyg.2023.1156661.

11 Brown, William M., Nathan S. Consedine, and Carol Magai. "Altruism Relates to Health in an Ethnically Diverse Sample of Older Adults." *The Journals of Gerontology: Series B* 60, no. 3 (May 1, 2005): P143–52. https://doi.org/10.1093/geronb/60.3.p143.

12 Max-Planck-Gesellschaft. "Helping Pays off: People Who Care for Others Live Longer," n.d. https://www.mpg.de/10873883/helping-pays-off-people-who-care-for-others-live-longer.

13 Kim, Eric S., Victor J. Strecher, and Carol D. Ryff. "Purpose in Life and Use of Preventive Health Care Services." *Proceedings of the National Academy of Sciences of the United States of America* 111, no. 46 (November 3, 2014): 16331–36. https://doi.org/10.1073/pnas.1414826111.

14 Hill, Patrick L., and Nicholas A. Turiano. 2014. "Purpose in Life as a Predictor of Mortality Across Adulthood." *Psychological Science*

25 (7): 1482–86. https://doi.org/10.1177/0956797614531799.

15   Bernacki, Matthew L., and Candance Walkington. "The Role of Situational Interest in Personalized Learning." Journal of Educational Psychology 110, no. 6 (August 1, 2018): 864–81. https://doi.org/10.1037/edu0000250.

16   Luke K. Fryer ad Mary Ainley. "Supporting Interest in a Study Domain: A Longitudinal Test of the Interplay Between Interest, Utility-value, and Competence Beliefs." *Learning and Instruction* 60 (April 1, 2019): 252–62. https://doi.org/10.1016/j.learninstruc.2017.11.002.

17   CollegeVine Blog. "The 10 Most Underrated Pre-Med Colleges in the U.S.," January 4, 2019. https://blog.collegevine.com/the-10-most-underrated-premed-colleges-in-the-us.

18   Schippers, Michaéla C., and Niklas Ziegler. 2019. "Life Crafting as a Way to Find Purpose and Meaning in Life." *Frontiers in Psychology* 10 (December). https://doi.org/10.3389/fpsyg.2019.02778.

19   Cascone, Sarah. "How Hard Is It to Make It as an Artist? A New Study Shows There Are Many Paths to Success—and Failure." *Artnet News*, June 12, 2018. https://news.artnet.com/art-world/artist-financial-stability-survey-1300895.

20   Costa, Paul T., and Robert R. McCrae. 1978. "Objective Personality Assessment." In The Clinical Psychology of Aging, edited by Martha Storandt, Ilene C. Siegler, and Merrill F. Elias, 119-143. Boston, MA: Springer US.

21   Stéphan, Yannick. "Openness to Experience and Active Older Adults' Life Satisfaction: A Trait and Facet-level Analysis." *Personality and Individual Differences* 47, no. 6 (October 1, 2009): 637–41. https://doi.org/10.1016/j.paid.2009.05.025.

22   Lüdtke, Oliver, Brent W. Roberts, Ulrich Trautwein, and Gabriel Nagy. "A Random Walk Down University Avenue: Life Paths,

Life Events, and Personality Trait Change at the Transition to University Life." *Journal of Personality and Social Psychology* 101, no. 3 (January 1, 2011): 620–37. https://doi.org/10.1037/a0023743.

23   Gregory, Tess, Ted Nettelbeck, and Carlene Wilson. "Openness to Experience, Intelligence, and Successful Ageing." *Personality and Individual Differences* 48, no. 8 (June 1, 2010): 895–99. https://doi.org/10.1016/j.paid.2010.02.017.

24   Ferguson, Eamonn, and Peter A. Bibby. "Openness to Experience and All-cause Mortality: A Meta-analysis and Requivalent From Risk Ratios and Odds Ratios." *British Journal of Health Psychology* 17, no. 1 (October 31, 2011): 85–102. https://doi.org/10.1111/j.2044-8287.2011.02055.x.

25   Yeager, David S., Marlone D. Henderson, David Paunesku, Gregory M. Walton, Sidney K. D'Mello, Brian James Spitzer, and Angela Duckworth. "Boring but Important: A Self-transcendent Purpose for Learning Fosters Academic Self-regulation." *Journal of Personality and Social Psychology* 107, no. 4 (October 1, 2014): 559–80. https://doi.org/10.1037/a0037637.

26   DeCaro, Marci S.., Robin D. Thomas, Neil B. Albert, and Sian L. Beilock. 2011. "Choking Under Pressure: Multiple Routes to Skill Failure." *Journal of Experimental Psychology: General* 140 (3): 390–406. https://doi.org/10.1037/a0023466

27   Vogel, Susanne, and Lars Schwabe. "Learning and Memory Under Stress: Implications for the Classroom." Npj Science of Learning 1, no. 1 (June 29, 2016). https://doi.org/10.1038/npjscilearn.2016.11.

28   Vine, Samuel J., and Mark R. Wilson. "Quiet Eye Training: Effects on Learning and Performance Under Pressure." *Journal of Applied Sport Psychology* 22, no. 4 (November 2, 2010): 361–76. https://doi.org/10.1080/10413200.2010.495106.

29   "The Luck Factor: Wiseman, Richard: 9780786869145: Amazon.

com: Books." n.d. https://www.amazon.com/Luck-Factor-Richard-Wiseman/dp/0786869143.

30 "Teach for America: 25 Years of Impact." 2023. Teach for America. December 14, 2023. https://www.teachforamerica.org/stories/teach-for-america-25-years-of-impact.

31 While there seems to be a gap in the literature regarding how Openness relates to career optionality, several studies touch on the idea including this one about the effects of extraversion and openness on career commitment.

32 Wortman, Jessica, Richard E. Lucas, and M. Brent Donnellan. 2012. "Stability and Change in the Big Five Personality Domains: Evidence From a Longitudinal Study of Australians." *Psychology and Aging* 27 (4): 867–74. https://doi.org/10.1037/a0029322

33 Hudson, Nathan W., and R. Chris Fraley. "Changing for the Better? Longitudinal Associations Between Volitional Personality Change and Psychological Well-Being." Personality and Social Psychology Bulletin 42, no. 5 (March 25, 2016): 603–15. https://doi.org/10.1177/0146167216637840.

34 Jackson, Joshua J., Patrick L. Hill, Brennan R. Payne, Brent W. Roberts, and Elizabeth a. L. Stine-Morrow. 2012. "Can an Old Dog Learn (and Want to Experience) New Tricks? Cognitive Training Increases Openness to Experience in Older Adults." *Psychology and Aging* 27 (2): 286–92. https://doi.org/10.1037/a0025918.

35 Allemand, Mathias, and Christoph Flückiger. 2017. "Changing Personality Traits: Some Considerations From Psychotherapy Process-outcome Research for Intervention Efforts on Intentional Personality Change." *Journal of Psychotherapy Integration* 27 (4): 476–94. https://doi.org/10.1037/int0000094.

36 "The Legacy of the 1965 Immigration Act." Center for Immigration Studies, 1 Sept. 1995, https://cis.org/Report/Legacy-1965-Immigration-Act. Accessed Feb 21, 2024.

37 "Clandestine Crossings: Migrants and Coyotes on the Texas-Mexico Border." 2009. *Www.Jstor.Org.* https://www.jstor.org/stable/10.7591/j.ctt7z8dn.

38 Pulles, Niels J., and Paul T. Hartman. 2017. "Likeability and Its Effect on Outcomes of Interpersonal Interaction." *Industrial Marketing Management* 66 (October): 56–63. https://doi.org/10.1016/j.indmarman.2017.06.008.

39 Feistauer, Daniela, and Tobias Richter. 2018. "Validity of Students' Evaluations of Teaching: Biasing Effects of Likability and Prior Subject Interest." *Studies in Educational Evaluation* 59 (December): 168–78. https://doi.org/10.1016/j.stueduc.2018.07.009.

40 Younan, Mariam, and Kristy A. Martire. 2021. "Likeability and Expert Persuasion: Dislikeability Reduces the Perceived Persuasiveness of Expert Evidence." Frontiers in Psychology 12 (December). https://doi.org/10.3389/fpsyg.2021.785677.

41 Hosoda, Megumi, Eugene F. Stone-Romero, and Gwen Coats. 2003. "THE EFFECTS OF PHYSICAL ATTRACTIVENESS ON JOB-RELATED OUTCOMES: A META-ANALYSIS OF EXPERIMENTAL STUDIES." *Personnel Psychology* 56 (2): 431–462. https://doi.org/10.1111/j.1744-6570.2003.tb00157.x.

42 Judge, Timothy A., and Daniel M. Cable. 2004. "The Effect of Physical Height on Workplace Success and Income: Preliminary Test of a Theoretical Model." *Journal of Applied Psychology* 89 (3): 428–441. https://doi.org/10.1037/0021-9010.89.3.428.

43 Gladstone, Gemma, and Gordon Parker. 2002. "When You're Smiling Does the Whole World Smile for You?" Australasian Psychiatry 10 (2): 144–46. https://doi.org/10.1046/j.1440-1665.2002.00423.x.

44 Beebe, Steven A. 1974. "Eye Contact: A Nonverbal Determinant of Speaker Credibility." *The Speech Teacher* 23 (1): 21–25.

https://doi.org/10.1080/03634527409378052.

45 Hitomi Tsujita and Jun Rekimoto, "Smiling Makes Us Happier: Enhancing Positive Mood and Communication with Smile-Encouraging Digital Appliances," in UbiComp '11: Proceedings of the 13th International Conference on Ubiquitous Computing (New York: ACM, 2011), 1-10, https://doi.org/10.1145/2030112.2030114.

46 Rosenthal, L. T. a. R. (1990). The nature of rapport and its nonverbal correlates. Psychological Inquiry, 1(4), 285–293. https://www.jstor.org/stable/1449345.

47 "Never Split the Difference: Negotiating as if Your Life Depended on It: Voss, Chris, Raz, Tahl: 9780062407801: Amazon.com: Books," n.d. https://www.amazon.com/Never-Split-Difference-Negotiating-Depended/dp/0062407805.

48 Bowles, Samuel, and Herbert Gintis. *A Cooperative Species. Princeton University Press eBooks*, 2011. https://doi.org/10.1515/9781400838837.

49 "The 11 Laws of Likability: Relationship Networking... Because People Do Business With People They Like: Michelle Tillis Lederman: 9780814416372: Amazon.com: Books." Michelle is a networking and communications expert with more than a decade of experience helping individuals and companies communicate better. Full disclosure, I've never even spoken to her—just read her book, and then connected with her on LinkedIn.

50 Wanberg, Connie R., Edwin a. J. Van Hooft, Songqi Liu, and Borbala Csillag. "Can Job Seekers Achieve More Through Networking? The Role of Networking Intensity, Self-efficacy, and Proximal Benefits." *Personnel Psychology* 73, no. 4 (January 15, 2020): 559–85. https://doi.org/10.1111/peps.12380.

51 Winerman, Lea. n.d. "Helping Men to Help Themselves." Https://Www.Apa.Org. https://www.apa.org/monitor/jun05/helping.

52 Zhao, Xuan, and Nicholas Epley. 2022. "Surprisingly Happy to Have Helped: Underestimating Prosociality Creates a Misplaced Barrier to Asking for Help." *Psychological Science* 33 (10): 1708–31. https://doi.org/10.1177/09567976221097615.

53 "The Law of Success (Deluxe Hardcover Book): Hill, Napoleon: 9789389157949: Amazon.com: Books." n.d. https://www.amazon.com/Law-Success-Napoleon-Hill/dp/9389157943/ref=tmm_hrd_swatch_0?_encoding=UTF8&qid=&sr=.

54 Granovetter, Mark S. 1973. "The Strength of Weak Ties." American Journal of Sociology 78 (6): 1360–80. https://www.jstor.org/stable/2776392.

55 Rajkumar, Karthik, Guillaume Saint-Jacques, Iavor Bojinov, Erik Brynjolfsson, and Sinan Aral. 2022. "A Causal Test of the Strength of Weak Ties." Science 377 (6612): 1304–10. https://doi.org/10.1126/science.abl4476.

56 "Cities and Ambition." n.d. https://www.paulgraham.com/cities.html.

57 Huberman, Andrew. 2023. "Tim Ferriss: How to Learn Better & Create Your Best Future | Huberman Lab Podcast." https://www.youtube.com/watch?v=doupx8SAs5Y.

58 Chase's injury was classified as an incomplete ASIA B injury affecting his C4—C7 vertebrae. "Prognosis and Goal Setting in Spinal Cord Injury." n.d. Physiopedia. https://www.physio-pedia.com/Prognosis_and_Goal_Setting_in_Spinal_Cord_Injury.

59 Lopez, Jason Kido, and Matthew J. Fuxjager. 2012. "Self-deception's Adaptive Value: Effects of Positive Thinking and the Winner Effect." Consciousness and Cognition 21 (1): 315–24. https://doi.org/10.1016/j.concog.2011.10.008.

60 Hatzigeorgiadis, Antonis, Nikos Zourbanos, Evangelos Galanis, and Yiannis Theodorakis. 2011. "Self-Talk and Sports Performance." Perspectives on Psychological Science 6 (4): 348–

56. https://doi.org/10.1177/1745691611413136.

61 Burch, Gerald F. 2014. "Experiential Learning—What Do We Know? A Meta-Analysis of 40 Years of Research." March 10, 2014. https://absel-ojs-ttu.tdl.org/absel/article/view/2127.

62 There are many competing experiential learning theories, some of which don't align with Kolb and a few go as far as criticizing his theories. That said, there is more supporting research around Kolb's theories than any other. "David A. Kolb." n.d. https://scholar.google.com/citations?user=MBn_GG4AAAAJ&hl=en&oi=ao.

63 Institute for Experiential Learning. 2024. "Kolb Experiential Learning Profile (KELP)—Individual Purchase—Institute for Experiential Learning." January 23, 2024. https://experientiallearninginstitute.org/product/kolb-experiential-learning-profile-kelp-individual-purchase/.

64 Robert Gemmell, Patrick Kanaley, and D. Leslie Kincaid, "Entrepreneurial Innovation as a Learning System," Journal of Enterprising Culture 26, no. 4 (2018): 489-503, https://www.researchgate.net/profile/Robert-Gemmell/publication/329005880_Entrepreneurial_Innovation_as_a_Learning_System/links/61254cf0169a1a010324b066/Entrepreneurial-Innovation-as-a-Learning-System.pdf.

65 Smith, Christopher D., and Damian Scarf. "Spacing Repetitions Over Long Timescales: A Review and a Reconsolidation Explanation." *Frontiers in Psychology* 8 (June 20, 2017). https://doi.org/10.3389/fpsyg.2017.00962.

66 Shakow, David. 1930. "Hermann Ebbinghaus." The American Journal of Psychology 42 (4): 505–18. https://doi.org/10.2307/1414874https://www.jstor.org/stable/1414874.

67 Cepeda, Nicholas J., Edward Vul, Doug Rohrer, John T. Wixted, and Harold Pashler. 2008. "Spacing Effects in Learning." *Psychological Science* 19 (11): 1095–1102. https://doi.

org/10.1111/j.1467-9280.2008.02209.x.

68 "Why We Sleep: Unlocking the Power of Sleep and Dreams: Walker PhD, Matthew: 9781501144318: Amazon.com: Books." n.d. https://www.amazon.com/Why-We-Sleep-Unlocking-Dreams/dp/1501144316.

69 Keller, Jan, Dominika Kwaśnicka, Patrick Klaiber, Lena Sichert, Phillippa Lally, and Lena Fleig. 2021. "Habit Formation Following Routine-based Versus Time-based Cue Planning: A Randomized Controlled Trial." *British Journal of Health Psychology* 26 (3): 807–24. https://doi.org/10.1111/bjhp.12504.

70 Maxwell Maltz, Psycho-Cybernetics (New York: Pocket Books, 1969), 1.

71 Keller, Jan, Dominika Kwaśnicka, Patrick Klaiber, Lena Sichert, Phillippa Lally, and Lena Fleig. 2021. "Habit Formation Following Routine-based Versus Time-based Cue Planning: A Randomized Controlled Trial." *British Journal of Health Psychology* 26 (3): 807–24. https://doi.org/10.1111/bjhp.12504.

72 Sword, Helen. 2016. "'Write Every Day!': A Mantra Dismantled." *International Journal for Academic Development* 21 (4): 312–22. https://doi.org/10.1080/1360144x.2016.1210153.

73 "Professors as Writers: A Self-Help Guide to Productive Writing: Boice, Robert: 9780913507131: Amazon.com: Books," n.d. https://www.amazon.com/Professors-Writers-Self-Help-Productive-Writing/dp/091350713X.

74 Mario Busto. "The Freedom of Ignorance- Orson Welles," September 3, 2020. https://www.youtube.com/watch?v=iiHeNyY629A.

75 Team, Nfi. "Deep Focus—Everything You Need to Know." NFI, April 24, 2023. https://www.nfi.edu/deep-focus/.

76 Kaiser, Cameron. 2024. "Palm OS and the Devices That Ran It:

An Ars Retrospective." Ars Technica. April 25, 2024. https://arstechnica.com/gadgets/2024/04/palm-os-and-the-devices-that-ran-it-an-ars-retrospective/.

77 "Handspring—Treo 600." n.d. Mobile Phone Museum. https://www.mobilephonemuseum.com/phone-detail/palm-treo-600.

78 Wikipedia contributors. 2024. "Reality Distortion Field." Wikipedia. May 30, 2024. https://en.wikipedia.org/wiki/Reality_distortion_field.

79 Richițeanu-Năstase, Elena Ramona, and Camelia Stăiculescu. 2019. "Are Extrovert People More Satisfied With Life? Case Study." *Mental Health* 1 (1): 68–70. https://doi.org/10.32437/mhgcj.v1i1.28.

80 Borkenau, Peter, and Anette Liebler. 1995. "Observable Attributesas Manifestations and Cues of Personality and Intelligence." *Journal of Personality* 63 (1): 1–25. https://doi.org/10.1111/j.1467-6494.1995.tb00799.x.

81 H, Mark, DO, and Amirali Minbashian. 2014. "A Meta-analytic Examination of the Effects of the Agentic and Affiliative Aspects of Extraversion on Leadership Outcomes." *The Leadership Quarterly* 25 (5): 1040–53. https://doi.org/10.1016/j.leaqua.2014.04.004.

82 Margolis, Seth, and Sonja Lyubomirsky. "Experimental Manipulation of Extraverted and Introverted Behavior and Its Effects on Well-being." *Journal of Experimental Psychology: General* 149, no. 4 (April 1, 2020): 719–31. https://doi.org/10.1037/xge0000668.

83 Yin, Yian, Yang Wang, James A. Evans, and Dashun Wang. "Quantifying the Dynamics of Failure Across Science, Startups and Security." *Nature* 575, no. 7781 (October 30, 2019): 190–94. https://doi.org/10.1038/s41586-019-1725-y.

84 Kellogg Insight. "Why Do Some People Succeed After Failing,

While Others Continue to Flounder?," April 19, 2022. https:// insight.kellogg.northwestern.edu/article/some-people-succeed-after-failing-others-flounder.

85 Carrington, Mary, Michael Dean, Maureen P. Martin, and Stephen J. O'Brien. "Genetics of HIV-1infection: Chemokine Receptor CCR5 Polymorphism and Its Consequences." *Human Molecular Genetics* 8, no. 10 (September 1, 1999): 1939–45. https://doi.org/10.1093/hmg/8.10.1939.

86 "NIH Data Book—Success Rates: R01-Equivalent and Research Project Grants." n.d. https://report.nih.gov/nihdatabook/category/10.

87 "Primary Lung Graft Dysfunction—UpToDate." n.d. UpToDate. https://www.uptodate.com/contents/primary-lung-graft-dysfunction.

88 "Amazon.com: Quit: The Power of Knowing When to Walk Away: 9780593422991: Duke, Annie: Books." n.d. https://www.amazon.com/Quit-Power-Knowing-When-Walk/dp/0593422996.

89 Wang, Yan, Benjamin F. Jones, and Dashun Wang. "Early-career Setback and Future Career Impact." *Nature Communications* 10, no. 1 (October 1, 2019). https://doi.org/10.1038/s41467-019-12189-3.

90 Ungar, Peter S. "Why We Have so Many Problems With Our Teeth." Scientific American, June 24, 2022. https://www.scientificamerican.com/article/why-we-have-so-many-problems-with-our-teeth/.

91 "Using Failures, Movement & Balance to Learn Faster—Huberman Lab," December 6, 2023. https://www.hubermanlab.com/episode/using-failures-movement-and-balance-to-learn-faster.

92 Linkenhoker, Brie A., and Eric I. Knudsen. "Incremental

Training Increases the Plasticity of the Auditory Space Map in Adult Barn Owls." *Nature* 419, no. 6904 (September 1, 2002): 293–96. https://doi.org/10.1038/nature01002.

93 "The Upside of Stress: Why Stress Is Good for You, and How to Get Good at It: McGonigal, Kelly: 9781101982938: Amazon.com: Books." n.d. https://www.amazon.com/Upside-Stress-Why-Good-You/dp/1101982934/ref=tmm_pap_swatch_0?_encoding=UTF8&qid=&sr=.

94 Keller, Abiola O., Kristin Litzelman, Lauren E. Wisk, Torsheika Maddox, Erika R. Cheng, Paul D. Creswell, and Whitney P. Witt. 2012. "Does the Perception That Stress Affects Health Matter? The Association With Health and Mortality." *Health Psychology* 31 (5): 677–84. https://doi.org/10.1037/a0026743.

95 Kumar, Shaina A., Madison E. Edwards, Hanna M. Grandgenett, Lisa L. Scherer, David DiLillo, and Anna E. Jaffe. 2022. "Does Gratitude Promote Resilience during a Pandemic? An Examination of Mental Health and Positivity at the Onset of COVID-19." Journal of Happiness Studies 23 (7): 3463–83. https://doi.org/10.1007/s10902-022-00554-x.

96 "Drive: The Surprising Truth About What Motivates Us: Pink, Daniel H.: 8601411029837: Amazon.com: Books." n.d. https://www.amazon.com/Drive-Surprising-Truth-About-Motivates/dp/1594488843/ref=tmm_hrd_swatch_0?_encoding=UTF8&qid=&sr=.

www.ingramcontent.com/pod-product-compliance
Lightning Source LLC
LaVergne TN
LVHW042249070526
838201LV00089B/85